To Ruth, Patti, Ann, Bill and Mike

ARMS CONTROL AND DISARMAMENT: SUCCESS OR FAILURE?

By
William F. Ansberry, Ph.D.
Associate Professor of Political Science
Southeast Missouri State

McCutchan Publishing Corporation
2526 Grove Street
Berkeley, California 94704

Library of Congress Catalog Card No. 78—98129
Standard Book No. 8211—0005-X

Preface

To some, the solution to the arms control race is simple. One group would have us believe that all that is necessary is to disarm unilaterally, thus encouraging other nations of the world to follow our example. A second group argues that the United States and the Western Powers should, under no circumstances, agree to any type of arms control until after the Soviet Union and her allies have completed the first stage of arms limitations.

Both of these extreme views fail to take into consideration the many problems related to the arms control and disarmament negotiations. This work is an attempt to study these problems and their effect upon past and present discussions.

I am especially grateful for the encouragement from my mother and late father, Michael C. Ansberry and also the late Major Charles M. Robertson.

Finally, I owe special thanks to my wife Ruth, and our children, Patti, Ann, Bill and Mike, for their patience, understanding, and encouragement which made the preparation of this book possible.

TABLE OF CONTENTS

CHAPTER I

INTRODUCTION AND BACKGROUND

Any study of the problems involving arms control and disarmament in the nation-state system must, of necessity, first survey previous efforts along these lines.

The term, "arms control," seems to imply that the nations of the world are engaged in an all-out economic effort to achieve military superiority. Hedley Bull points out the fallacy in this. Arms competition between the United States and the Soviet Union is no exception. The resources each has allocated to the amassing of military power have been deliberately limited.[1]

It is not necessarily true that an arms race always increases the prospect of war. Sometimes, failure of one side to keep pace in such a race is more detrimental to world peace than the arms race itself. Because of this, the relevance of an arms race to world stability and to the risks of war cannot be mechanically stated. Much will depend upon the specifics of the international situation, especially upon whether the opposing states are adequately deterred at the existing level of armaments.

A widespread belief in the world today is the view that world peace depends entirely upon general and complete disarmament. Any serious consideration of general and complete disarmament must lead to a study of the problems of world government. Nuclear disarmament discussions carry the same implications. At the same time, limited arms control agreements, such as the "hot line," the Nuclear Test Ban Treaty, and the Non-Proliferation Treaty signify a continuation of the bipolar world in which we have been accustomed to living in the post World War II period.[2]

Early Attempts at Arms Control and Disarmament

The possibility of achieving this state of disarmament is no closer today than it has been throughout the history of arms control discussions and negotiations. Nations will not disarm unless other aspects of their security and welfare can be protected in a disarming and a disarmed world.

The Clark-Sohn plan is an attempt to show the states of the world that their economic, social, and security interests can be carried on in a safer and more effective manner in a disarmed world than under the conditions that exist today.[3] The states of the world are urged to disarm by appealing to national self-interest on a broader basis than simply asking for abolishment of military capacity in the face of the dangers of nuclear war.

1

In disarmament or arms control negotiations, the tension is increased by the tendency of the powerful states to emphasize their strength as the realistic bases for bargaining while the less powerful insist upon sovereign equality as the basis for bargaining.

As an analysis of the negotiations will show later in this work, the suggestion that equality must either precede arms control or be reached shortly after the start of the process has been one of the major road blocks to agreement. Does equality refer to the overall military strength or does it refer to each major category of weapons? Is it possible to maintain the same military advantage or disadvantage during the arms control or disarmament process that existed prior to the start of the program? Thus far, questions such as these have not been answered to the satisfaction of the world's nations.

Under these conditions, it is unlikely that any form of drastic disarmament is possible in the near future. Fear that the other side will cheat in the absence of a satisfactory substitute for trust; differing concepts of security during the arms control process; inability to fulfill foreign goals in a disarmed world, and reluctance to give up national strength to achieve national security—all of these center around the issue of confidence, reliability, and self-interest.

In a world which consists of over 120 sovereign states (according to the United Nations estimate) any arms control or disarmament approach which advocates the general and complete elimination of armaments is doomed to failure, the same fate which such methods have met throughout history. When viewing the arms control problems that have faced the nations of the world over the years, it will be noted that those Rush-Bagot solutions which met with any form of acceptance, such as the Rush-Bagot Treaty of 1818 or the Test-Ban Treaty of 1963, were the least comprehensive in nature. By advocating the partial or limited measure approach, several plans involving different areas of arms control could be put forth. This creates a situation in which most nations will find parts of the proposals acceptable to their national interest. It also presents a situation in which bargaining among nations can take place. Under any comprehensive plan for arms control and disarmament, states are faced with an "all or nothing at all" condition. Using the partial approach, a nation may accept parts of different plans put forth while rejecting others. In this manner, steps may be taken, however slowly, toward more comprehensive arms control agreements.

There have been more than 1,600 arms races since 650 B.C., with one nation or empire trying to make bigger and better weapons than everyone else. Only one in a hundred of these arms build-ups has not ended in war. Some Chinese states made a disarmament treaty as early as the sixth century B.C. In the Chinese Age of Confusion, two northern Hwang Ho states formed a union to make war against one of the Yangtse Valley states. Following the successful conquest by the Hwang Ho states, a treaty providing for general disarmament was formulated. This treaty kept the peace for a hundred years.[4]

Today the world is engaged in the deadliest arms race of all times. With the latest nuclear tipped missiles, it is estimated that 300 million people could be killed in one hour.

The germ of disarmament can be traced to individual peace plans advocated by such men as Jean Bodin (1571), William Penn (1685), the Abbe de Saint-Pierre (1713), Jean Jacques Rousseau (1756), Jeremy Bentham (1789) and Immanuel Kant (1795). These philosophers and statesmen envisaged a society in which large armaments would be unnecessary.[5]

The problems brought about by arms buildup were not only being discussed in Europe at this period. In America, Washington, Jefferson and Franklin also looked upon the enormous armaments of Europe as folly. Washington, in his farewell address, spoke with deep feeling of the danger of enormous armaments to democracy. "Overgrown military establishments are, under any form of government, inauspicious to liberty and are regarded as particularly hostile to republican liberty."[6]

The first modern attempt at disarmament occurred in 1816 when Czar Alexander I of Russia proposed to Britain the simultaneous reduction of all armed forces. The post-Napoleonic period was marked by an attempt at international organization which was inspired by the Czar's idealistic Holy Alliance and also by the diplomatic agreement for sustaining the system established by the Treaty of Vienna. This system soon lost the backing of Great Britain because of the inability to distinguish between international and domestic questions and also because of its policy to assist the Hapsburg princes in claiming to continue their authority by divine right in Spain and Italy.[7]

The Treaty of Vienna (1815) also added a new principle, the Concert of Europe, to the two recognized principles, the public law of Europe and the balance of power. Under this principle, the great powers were to consult before changes in the public law of Europe could become valid.[8] It was hoped that such an approach might prevent hostilities.

Despite the favorable dispositions of the governments and the exhaustion of European nations after twenty-five years of war, the question was not seriously considered. Metternich and the British were suspicious of Russia. Alexander was interested in expanding Russia's influence into Eastern Europe and Europe in general was afraid of French militarism.

The term "disarmament" has many meanings. Penal destruction or reduction of armaments of a country defeated in war is one concept of the term which has been enforced since ancient times and as recently as World War I and World War II.

Bilateral disarmament agreements applying to specific geographic areas is another meaning for which the term disarmament has been used. An example of this usage is the Rush-Bagot Agreement between Great Britain and the United States, which, since 1817, has kept the Great Lakes and the United States--Canadian border disarmed.[9] This was the only voluntary and mutual disarmament achievement of the nineteenth century.

Peace enthusiasts often refer to this treaty as an example of successful disarmament which should be copied by the world powers today. Such a comparison of the 1817-1818 period to the world situation today fails to take into consideration the differences in geographic, political, economic and strategic factors. Following the War of 1812, policies of Great Britain and the United States were not in conflict. Therefore, each could agree to a limitation of armaments on the Great Lakes at a saving in expenditures and without sacrificing their national interests. The Rush-Bagot Treaty, then, is another example which shows that agreement on disarmament and armament issues is possible only when the policies of states do not clash.

Most of the attempts at securing international peace through disarmament have failed. The two which succeeded, the Rush-Bagot Agreement, mentioned above, and the Washington Treaty for the Limitation of Naval Armaments of 1922, were an integral part of a political settlement which carried in itself the assurance of peace. In other words, as the armaments race is a symptom of political conflict which is likely to lead to war, so is disarmament the symptom of the disappearance of political tension which, by itself, gives assurance for the preservation of peace.[10] Diplomacy alone, especially if it is of the local and qualitative types, gives no such assurance. At best, it would only be able to alter the methods by which war is to be waged, but not the incidence of war itself.

Pre-World War I Efforts: The Hague Conferences

Most of the arguments advanced today for an arms control and disarmament program were also advanced during the period of the Hague Conferences. Some of the arguments being voiced by advocates of disarmament were: (1) armaments were increasing the likelihood and barbarity of war; (2) funds and energies could better be devoted to more beneficial purposes; and (3) all mankind yearned for a better way to settle world conflicts.

Just as many of the arguments put forth to justify a disarmament program at the turn of the century are still heard today, many of the same difficulties that faced the statesman of that period remain for present negotiations. One of the major problems then, as now, arose when it became necessary to find a formula for combining disarmament with the principles of international law.

Another problem, which was never settled, dealt with sovereignty. When establishing an inspection system or when the application of sanctions are voted by an international body, how can these be carried forward without interfering with national sovereignty? Secondly, to what extent should inspections or sanctions be allowed to interfere with national sovereignty if such an infringement is to be allowed?

Before any of the above problems could be solved, it would first be necessary to define the exact nature of armament. Materials which are considered by some nations as top priority armaments will be considered by other nations as only slightly related to the disarmament negotiation. War and industrial progress are closely related. Because of this, it is impossible to reduce military expenditure in many areas without reducing expenditures in other industrial areas. However, any "production lag" brought about by disarmament agreements among nations, would postpone and possibly even prevent war in a short run period. If such a treaty were honored until a war began, which is highly unlikely, it would be years before the relative strength could be greatly altered. A treaty that merely establishes rules of war creates no "production lag."[11] As soon as a war begins, the armaments are available. It is a simple matter to use these arms in violation of treaty agreements.[12]

The emphasis at the First Hague Conference was on regulation of armaments and war and not on their abolition. Russian arms limitations proposals advanced at the conference, which would have prevented increases in troop levels or military and naval budgets, met with no success. The Conference also defeated proposals which would have eliminated use of any new explosives, new inventions in field artillery and automatic weapons, and would have prevented changes in existing types of small arms or make use of automatic weapons.

The First Hague Conference met from May 18 to July 29, 1899. Twenty-six of the fifty-nine sovereign states of the world were represented by nearly one hundred delegates. Each nation was permitted to send as many delegates as it wished, but each was to have only one vote. Included among the twenty-six states were: twenty European states; four Asiatic states, China, Japan, Persia, and Siam; and two American states, the United States and Mexico.

The conference was presided over by M. de Staal, the Russian Ambassador to London. Three committees were created to deal with the major topics. The first dealt with the limitation of armaments and war budgets. The second committee was concerned with the extension of the Geneva Red Cross rules of 1864 and 1868 to maritime warfare. The third committee considered mediation, arbitration and other methods of preventing armed conflicts.[13]

Discussion of the limitation of armaments began June 23. As mentioned previously, disarmament was not to be the topic of consideration. The only positive result of these discussions was the creation of the Hague Court of Arbitration.[14] However, none of the participating nations was willing to bind itself to a fast rule to submit all questions to arbitration. Lord Salisbury felt that the court should deal only with minor disputes, especially cases dealing with claims for money compensation, and not with the more important political questions.

Germany was even more strongly opposed to such a court than Great Britain. Rather than being responsible for the break-up of the conference, the German delegate agreed to the establishment of a permanent court of arbitration on the condition that each state would have final say in each case as to whether or not to resort to the court for a decision.

Captain Mahan, the American Naval delegate, worked very closely with Sir

John Fisher, the British Naval delegate to the Conference. Both Mahan and Fisher had little sympathy with the main purposes of the Conference; however, opposition by the German delegates relieved other representatives of the task of rejecting the Russian proposals.

The great powers found these proposals of the Czar most troublesome to their plans for the future. Most of these powers, however, were forced to go through the motions of trying to reach some sort of agreement on arms limitation, because of public opinion both at home and abroad.

In spite of the adoption of a plan for the Court of Arbitration, plus other minor agreements mentioned previously, the First Hague Conference did little toward solving the problem of disarmament.

The Second Hague Conference met from June 15 to October 18, 1907. At the suggestion of President Roosevelt, the Latin American countries were also invited to the conference. Forty-four sovereign states sent delegations to the Hague, an increase of eighteen over the number of nations represented at the First Hague Conference.

The British delegate suggested that the conference confirm the resolution adopted by the preceding conference of 1899 in regard to the limitation of military expenditures. In the absence of the German delegate, the resolution was accepted unanimously. Thus, the matter of arms limitation was disposed of in less than half an hour, with the adoption of a resolution which stated that it was desirable that the governments should resume the serious examination of the limitation of military expenditures.[15]

Even though the Hague Conferences failed in the areas of disarmament and arbitration, advances were made in revising the rules of warfare and prohibiting the use of certain types of weapons. The effectiveness of these agreements, however, is subject to debate, since all were violated in both World Wars.

Hague Conferences Evaluated

The failure of the Hague Conferences to reach any sort of armament limitation agreement once again illustrated how closely related the disarmament question is to the political problems facing the world. Any type of arms limitation agreement which is reached by the powers of the world must first be preceded by settlement of the major political problems existing among these nations. Only when the national policies of the world's leading powers are not in conflict will it be possible to devise a meaningful plan for armament reduction.

Disarmament proposals put forth at the Hague Conferences, as well as those we have viewed prior to 1898, failed because few of the nations involved seriously considered arms control or disarmament. As has been shown throughout these early attempts at disarmament, it would be impossible as well as foolhardy to attempt to place the blame for the failure of the conferences at the doorstep of any single nation.

Even though few agreements were reached at the Hague meetings, and many of those that were approved were later broken during the World War I period, a beginning had been made toward some sort of world organization. For the first time, the principle of universality began to emerge. Included in the forty-four nations attending the Second Hague Conference were not only those from Europe, the seat of world power during the nineteenth century, but also nations from other areas, such as Latin America. Inis Claude called the Second Hague Conference the world's first real general assembly.[16]

From the above, and the examples cited, it is obvious that the participating nations had little or no interest in a general and complete plan for arms control. With each nation working for the advantage, at the expense of the other nations, it is clear that only in the partial or limited approach to the arms control and disarmament problem was there any possibility of reaching agreement. This is also true today—general and complete disarmament would necessitate a complete revision of the long range national security goals of the major powers, whereas limited measures will necessitate only minor changes in these long range goals of the participating nations.

FOOTNOTES

[1]Hedley Bull, *The Control of the Arms Race*, New York: Praeger, 1965, pp. 14–15.

[2]Alastair Buchan (ed.), *A World of Nuclear Power?* Englewood Cliffs, N. J., 1966, p. 3.

[3]See *Current Disarmament Proposals* New York: World Law Fund, 1964, p. 61.

[4]Quincy, Wright, *Limitation of Armament*, New York: Institute of International Education, 1921, p. 9.

[5]Quincy, Wright, *The Role of International Law in the Elimination of War*, New York: Oceana Publications Inc., 1961, p. 25.

[6]Edwin D. Mead, *Washington, Jefferson and Franklin on War*, Boston: World Peace Foundation, 1913, p. 10.

[7]Quincy, Wright, *A Study of War*, Vol. I: Chicago: University of Chicago Press, 1943, p. 338.

[8]*Ibid.*, p. 362. Also see Nicolson, Sir Harold G., *The Congress of Vienna: A Study of Allied Unity, 1812–1822*, New York: Harcourt, Brace and Company, 1946.

[9]Samuel Flagg Bemis, *A Diplomatic History of the United States*, New York: Henry Holt and Company, 1936, pp. 172–173.

[10]U. S., Congress, Senate, Subcommittee of the Committee on Foreign Relations, *Hearings, Control and Reduction of Armaments*, 85th Cong., 1st Sess., 1957, pp. 1091–1092.

[11]The time needed to convert industry to arms production.

[12]Wright, *A Study of War*, II, p. 799.

[13]Merze Tate, *The Disarmament Illusion: The Movement for a Limitation of Armaments to 1907*, New York: Macmillian Co., 1942, p. 279.

[14]Stephen S. Fenishell and Phillip Andrews, *The United States: Blueprint for Peace*, Philadelphia: John C. Winston Company, 1951, p. 31.

[15]Collier, p. 3.

[16]Claude, Jr., Inis L., *Swords into Plowshares*, New York: Random House, 1956, p. 29.

CHAPTER II
THE POST-WORLD WAR I PERIOD:
THE LEAGUE OF NATIONS

Detailed discussions of arms control negotiations make two points clear: (1) since the first Hague Conference of 1899, technical developments have increasingly convinced statesmen that armament competition is dangerous to international peace, to national security and indeed, since World War II, to the survival of civilization; and (2) substantial agreement among the great powers on disarmament is impossible so long as each of them suspects the others of aggressive intentions. The objectives of arms control proposals have, in fact, been the same as that of national arms building programs—to improve the relative power position of the proposing nation, on the assumption that successful diplomacy requires negotiation from a position of superior strength.

The unreality of arms control negotiations is suggested by the tendency of the great powers to change their positions when agreement seems within the realm of possibility. During the League period, the United States opposed effective international inspection and control. During the same period, the Soviet Union was a leading advocate of a thorough inspection and control system. Today, the United States and the Soviet Union have taken reverse positions. Even so, the paths of these two nations were parallel during the early days of the League. Both remained outside of the organization and both preferred to pursue a purely national path. When the Soviet Union was admitted to the League, her attitude was that arms control should pose no major problem. All that was necessary was to start scrapping military equipment. At the same time the United States, disregarding the Covenant of the League of Nations, the Treaty of Guarantee, the Protocal and the Locorno Pact, was saying abolish war. This could be accomplished simply by signing a pact.

Efforts to find an acceptable program for the regulation of armaments, as well as a plan of disarmament suitable to the world's leading powers, proved to be nearly as impossible as in the earlier periods of history. Attempts to find solutions to the many problems concerning disarmament were made both within the framework of the League of Nations and outside of the League. Although looking at these difficulties within the context of the post World War I period, it becomes increasingly evident that most of these same problems still exist today, along with many new ones which have resulted from the nuclear era.

The idea of reducing armaments could not appeal equally to all nations. Each nation was in a different stage of developing a colonial empire. Those countries which lagged behind in the drive for overseas possessions, chiefly because they were not united until the latter part of the nineteenth century, were not willing to accept the status quo at the beginning of the twentieth century.

National prestige or nationalism also proved to be a serious obstacle. Today, as in the period following World War I, the world tends to estimate nations according to their military power. As better communication systems were developed and the world powers were brought close together, this factor became even more important. Action by any nation in the world had an effect upon the other nations.

Arms Control Problems: Possible Solutions

Throughout the history of disarmament there have been many schools of thought as to the major causes of war and how these causes could best be eliminated. Two of the arguments most frequently heard, the points of view of the realist and the pacifist, were heard in the period following World War I as well as today.

The pacifist point of view maintains that armaments are the cause of wars. International tension and political problems are made more difficult to solve by the arms race and high levels of armaments. As long as high armament stockpiles exist, there is the possibility that governments will resort to the use of them or that war could start because of human or mechanical error.[1] The conclusion of this view of the problem is that safety lies in immediate disarmament.

The complete abolition of armed forces would not necessarily have the desired results for which the pacifists hope. The need for national purposes, as well as the possible need for United Nations action, must also be taken into consideration.

Instead of increasing the sense of security, this approach would foster a feeling of greater insecurity. In such a world, nations industrially and economically powerful would be able to rearm with much greater ease than the poorer, less developed nations. In the absence of a powerful, well organized world community, no general disarmament plan is possible.

The realist viewpoint, on the other hand, maintains that wars are the cause of armaments; that nations would not arm if they were not afraid of war. Nations, therefore, arm themselves because of international tensions. Under these conditions disarmament would be feasible only when progress is made in solving the basic political problems which cause nations to arm themselves. Among this group, some also contend that it may even be dangerous to have a relaxation of tension, which would bring about steps toward disarmament, as long as underlying political problems remained unsolved. Hitler's rise to power is often used as an example.

Until 1870, when the German states were unified, the nineteenth century nations maintained small standing armies. This was true primarily because disputes that arose at this time were of a local nature. Following the unification of Germany, disputes that developed, such as the one between Germany and France over Alsace-Lorraine, involved a larger area and more of the world's major powers.[2] From the above, it would seem that the level of armament itself does not necessarily produce tension among nations. It would seem rather to point out the fallacy of the pacifist view that armaments are the cause, rather than the reflection of world conflicts.

If armaments are not the cause but the effect of wars, it follows that, according to this doctrine, the remedy for armaments lies in finding a way to abolish war. This presupposes the existence of a world community with the power to enforce international law. Any declaration outlawing war which allows each state to define a war in which it is engaged as defensive war is worthless. No nation is going to give up its right to self-defense.

Armaments are not only instruments for carrying on warfare. Actually, armaments are as important and possibly even more important during peace time than during times of war. Under these conditions, the controllers of armaments become the diplomats rather than the soldiers. The true head of the military is the foreign minister rather than the military chiefs.[3] From the above, it becomes evident that no disarmament is possible until an alternative instrument of policy is devised. By the same reasoning, no reduction of armament is possible as long as armament plays a key role in the foreign policy of the nation. The Clausewitzian theory, that war is an extension of the foreign policy of a nation, is not as easily explained today as it might have been in the past. War itself is not easy to define. In today's world it becomes necessary for the writer to be more exact, more descriptive, when referring to warfare. Secretary of Defense Robert McNamara, in a speech in Montreal, pointed out that in the past eight years there have been more than 150 significant international outbreaks of violence, each of which was serious enough to be designed as a challenge to the authority or the existence of the government in question.[4] From this, we see that today, conflicts which in the past would have been considered wars, are more often undeclared wars of the type referred to by Clausewitz. Even Walter Millis and James Real in their work, *The Abolition of War,* whose major argument is that a demilitarized world is a practical possibility, do not completely rule out wars, riots and disturbances, in the form of Wars of National Liberation.[5]

Two aspects of the disarmament approach which must also be reviewed are the quantitative as well as the qualitative reduction of armament. In past disarmament discussions, the quantitative reduction has occupied a central position. It has involved attempts to limit or reduce both manpower and equipment without drastically changing the existing situation. This problem of ratio was given a great deal of attention in the early discussions of the League's Preparatory Commission of the Disarmament Conference.

Important considerations for the ratio were: (1) size of populations; (2)

military potential of each state; (3) maintenance of the status quo; (4) geographic location of countries; (5) size and nature of maritime communications; (6) development of rail facilities; (7) frontier defense positions; (8) the special position of countries with professional armies; (9) the special position of agricultural countries without developed industries; and (10) the security offered to a state in case of attack by the provisions of the Covenant of the League.[6]

The size of the population was considered the most important by most experts. Not only would this be the chief factor in the building of regular military units, but the number of recruits available for conscription during times of emergencies must also be taken into consideration. Little or no agreement was reached on this topic, mainly because of disagreement on whether trained reserves should be counted when formulating plans for the reduction of the military within each nation. Maintenance of the status quo proved to be one of the most difficult points upon which to reach agreement. Since the size of the military forces that each nation would need would depend upon an estimate of the power needed to obtain its goals as well as to promote its own national security, it would seem that an agreement as to the maintenance of the status quo as the ratio of armaments would not be too difficult to reach. This, however, did not prove to be a true assumption. Some states were willing to discuss the relative strength as of 1927, others wanted to use the year 1913 as the basis for agreement while still others preferred the armament ratio that existed in 1900. Insofar as quantitative disarmament is concerned, the ratio seemed to be the central problem.

The question of qualitative disarmament led to discussions over whether professional or conscript forces were the more defensive in nature. Following World War I, there seemed to be a reasonable amount of agreement that long term professional armies were less dangerous to peace than conscript forces.

After the defeat of Germany, France's chief aim was to see that Germany was disarmed and that her state of armament remained at the lowest possible point. In the end, the argument over qualitative disarmament in the field of manpower developed into a duel between Germany and France.

Germany argued that control of the type of armament was the most practical way to bring about arms control regulations. France felt that tactical organization was more important than types of weapons. To France, the greatest danger to world peace came from the combination of a professional army nucleus with a large pool of conscript reserves available for quick mobilization. To France, colonial regulars should not be classed as part of the offensive strength of the nation.

Discussion of qualitative disarmament would not be complete without including a look at the suggestion for an international police force. If a functioning force could have been established, the size of national police forces could have been reduced. It was clear, however, that any such force would require a world organization different from that created following World War I.

France especially was interested in this aspect of possible disarmament approaches since she constantly worried about an attack by Germany.

Following the war, there was great interest in outlawing offensive weapons. By 1932, thirty countries had declared themselves in favor of some form of qualitative restriction. During the early 1930's, the list of nations reached forty-two. The great stumbling block to this approach came when an attempt was made to distinguish between offensive and defensive weapons. Under some conditions, a weapon might be used in a defensive capacity; however, under a set of different circumstances, the same weapon could be considered offensive in nature. When the Disarmament Conference convened in 1932, it became evident that no acceptable agreement could be reached on this problem. As Henry W. Forbes pointed out, "Churchill's disarmament fable serves as a worthy conclusion to the treatment of qualitative disarmament."[7]

In light of past history, it seems doubtful that arms control measures can be realized under conditions of extreme international tension. Nations that suspect one another of hostile intentions will naturally be unwilling to accept proposals put forth by their would-be enemy. Any agreement on major arms control or disarmament proposals will require a considerable measure of mutual trust as the first essential for such an agreement. As long as there is no drastic change, and international relations continue to rest on an unstable balance of military power among conflicting states, there will be no possibility for the success of any type of comprehensive arms control agreement.

Competition in armament is interwoven with political tension. Under these conditions, international agreement on an arms control formula is possible only when the national policies of states are not in conflict. This is true because international disarmament standardizes the relative diplomatic power of the nations involved and prevents the use of competition in armament to upset the political equilibrium.

Disarmament proposals failed in the post World War I period because no state seriously believed that an arms control or disarmament program was possible under existing conditions. No one nation was responsible for the competition in armaments. It must also be noted that no nation was completely innocent either, because each lived in a perpetual state of mutual fear and antagonism, expecting war at any time and always preparing for it. Many questions in Europe and throughout the world remained unsettled. No power was willing to face the future inadequately armed to protect its vital interests. These nations considered any proposal to limit armament as a device to give the inefficient countries an artificial position which they did not deserve in the family of nations.

Disarmament programs which attempt to fix ratios on armaments—the approach used throughout history, including the post World War I period—are bound to end in failure. This is true because they presuppose that nations must go on fighting. Nations will continue to fight until they either find a satisfactory substitute for war or realize that war in today's world threatens the destruction of that world.

The pacifist's view that if nations would agree to arbitrate and believe in the inviolability of the agreement, is an illusion in a world of nation-states. No great power is willing to submit all its differences, regardless of their justifiability, to international adjudication. Most states prefer to fight rather than surrender their vital interests. Arbitration is not applicable when the very existence of a state is involved or where its relative position in the community of nations is concerned. Major powers are willing only to arbitrate legal disputes. Normally, these powers insist that political issues cannot be judicially adjusted. Non-justifiable disputes are usually concerned with matters of national honor and vital issues. Clearly then, arbitration must be regarded as an aid to diplomacy, and not a substitute for it.

As a result of the absence of the United States from the League of Nations, France lost the British-American guarantee which President Wilson and Prime Minister Lloyd-George had offered as an inducement to a more conciliatory attitude toward Germany. This condition led France to emphasize security, guarantee, and sanctions which dominated the French position from 1919.[8] She proceeded, from this point, to substitute a network of treaties with her European allies for the legal process established by the League of Nations.

From the above, it becomes obvious that the insurance of security has remained the chief purpose of arms control negotiations. Since armaments and military personnel serve to establish national security, any disarmament scheme must provide for comprehensive security through other means.

FOOTNOTES

[1]Ellen C. Collier, *Disarmament: Historical Background and a Discussion of its Feasibility,* Library of Congress Legislative Reference Service Circular No. UA17 (Washington: U.S. Government Printing Office, 1960), p. 8.

[2]Henry A. Kiesinger, Jr., "Disarmament: Illusion and Reality," *American Strategy for the Nuclear Age,* ed. Walter F. Hahn and John C. Neff, (Garden City: Doubleday and Co., 1960), pp. 313–314.

[3]Salvador De Madariaga, *Disarmament* (New York: Coward-McConn, Inc., 1929), p. 59.

[4]James M. Gavin, "Military Power: The Limits of Persuasion," *Saturday Review,* XLIX, July 30, 1966, p. 19.

[5]Walter Millis and James Real, *The Abolition of War,* New York: Macmillan Co., 1963, p. 203.

[6]Henry W. Forbes, *The Strategy of Disarmament,* Washington D.C.: Public Affairs Press, 1962, p. 15.

[7]Each nation felt that its armaments were defensive in nature while other armaments were of the offensive type.

"Once upon a time all the animals in the zoo decided that they would disarm, and they arranged to have a conference to arrange the matter. So the rhinoceros said when we opened the proceedings that the use of teeth was barbarous and horrible and ought to be strictly prohibited by general consent. Horns, which were mainly defensive weapons, would of course, have to be allowed. The buffalo, the stag, the porcupine and even the little hedgehog all said they would vote with the rhino, but the lion and the tiger took a different view. They defended teeth and even claws, which they described as honorable weapons of immemorial antiquity. The panther, the leopard, the puma, and the whole tribe of small cats all supported the lion and the tiger. Then the bear spoke. He proposed that both teeth and horns should be banned and never used again for fighting by any animals. It would be quite enough if animals were allowed to give each other a good hug when they quarreled. No one objected to that. It was so fraternal, and it would be a great step toward peace. However, all the other animals were very offended with the bear, and the turkey fell into a perfect panic.

The discussion got so hot and angry, and all those animals began thinking so much about horns and teeth and hugging when they argued about peaceful intentions that had brought them together that they began to look at one another in a very nasty way. Luckily the keepers were able to calm them down and persuade them to go back quietly to their cages, and they began to feel quite friendly with one another again."

[8] De Madariaga, *Disarmament*, p. 80.

CHAPTER III

THE POST-WORLD WAR II PERIOD:

THE UNITED NATIONS

League of Nations Covenant-United Nations Charter

One of the reasons for the League of Nation's failure to develop a workable disarmament program was the one-sided approach taken by that body. While striving for technical agreements, the connected political problems were all but forgotten. Even so, it would be a mistake to look upon the League's efforts in the field of disarmament as a complete failure. Major General George V. Strong, who served as the chief military adviser to the United States delegation during the League of Nations Disarmament Conference, stated that the technical phase of the League's work was thorough enough to serve as a background to United Nations efforts in the field of disarmament.[1]

When the United Nations came into existence in 1945, it was not felt that the disarmament question would play a dominant role in the early stages of the organization. The Covenant of the League had placed the disarmament issue in a position of great importance, whereas the United Nations Charter implied that disarmament was to be an eventual goal rather than a topic for immediate discussion.[2] The Covenant more precisely emphasized disarmament, while the Charter emphasized collective security. Obligations found in the Covenant dealing with disarmament were more binding on member nations than those of the post World War II United Nations. Article 1 made willingness to accept the regulation of armament a stipulation for joining the League of Nations.[3] In addition to the above guarantees, member nations "shall accept regulations as may be prescribed by the League in regard to its military, naval, air forces, and armaments."[4]

Article 8 stated that the Council was responsible for formulating plans for the reduction of armaments which were to be presented to member nations for consideration. These plans were to be reconsidered and, if necessary, revised at least every ten years. A permanent commission was created by Article 9 to advise the Council on the execution of Articles 1 and 8 and other matters dealing with military and disarmament questions.

Under the Charter of the United Nations, disarmament was to be an eventual goal, rather than an immediate objective for the world peace organization. Later events, however, especially the development of nuclear weapons, moved the disarmament discussions into a position of primary importance, rather than the secondary role which had been foreseen in the Charter. This was true because,

15

with the advent of nuclear weapons, the difference between defeat or victory was measured in hours rather than months or years. The United Nations Charter did not make the willingness to agree to armament controls a price for membership in the organization. In fact, the word "disarmament" does not appear in the Charter until Article 11.

Even though the United Nations Charter emphasized arms control to a lesser extent than the Covenant of the League of Nations, efforts devoted to the area of disarmament have been much greater during the post-World War II period. The United States and the Soviet Union, the two most powerful nations to emerge from World War II, played a relatively small role in the disarmament efforts of the League of Nations. Great Britain was the champion of immediate disarmament agreements. France insisted upon an improvement of relations among the world's top powers prior to the acceptance of any disarmament plan.

Following Hitler's rise to power in 1933, the Soviet Union, represented by Maxim Litvinov, became the chief proponent of vigorous supervision. While advocating strict supervision, Litvinov failed to outline any details of the proposed inspection plan. During this period, the United States looked upon any type of inspection system with skepticism. Secretary of State Frank Kellogg stated, in 1926, that any arms limitations must depend upon the good faith of the participating nations.[5] By the time United Nations disarmament discussions were underway, the positions of the United States and the Soviet Union had practically been reversed. The United States now insists that no comprehensive disarmament plan is possible without an inspection system to verify the steps taken by each nation. The Soviet Union, on the other hand, feels that the first step must be disarmament itself. Once this has been accomplished, or at least a good start made in that direction, then the discussions on an inspection system can begin.

The United Nations profited from the lessons learned from the League. Collective security was recognized as one of the most important aspects of a disarmament program. Articles dealing with collective security reached their peak in Article 43 which states that

> all members of the United Nations, in order to contribute to the maintenance of international peace and security, undertake to make available to the Security Council, on its call and in accordance with a special agreement or agreements, armed forces, assistance, and facilities, including rights of passage, necessary for the purpose of maintaining international peace and security.[6]

There was, however, no agreement on how this was to be carried out. Although all the powers represented at the Dumbarton Oaks Conference agreed that sufficient military forces should be placed at the command of the Security Council, they differed as to how these forces should be organized.

Even though the disarmament talks following both World War I and World

War II have been unsuccessful, there were great contrasts between the two periods. The discussions after the second World War have been marked by a clear-cut difference of opinion between two power blocs, a condition which did not exist in the League of Nations period. Although both sides apparently agree that the question of limiting armaments must be considered together with problems of security and inspection, there has been very little agreement as to how this can be accomplished.

The major difference between earlier periods of history and today is that the disarmament problems have been complicated by the advent of nuclear weaponry. The opposing views on such problems as general disarmament, step by step measures, defining armaments, national sovereignty, inspection and control have kept the disarmament negotiations deadlocked during these years.

The Atomic Energy Commission of the United Nations

In 1943, two years before the end of World War II, the United States, the United Kingdom and Canada decided on a joint effort in atomic energy. Top level consultations took place between President Roosevelt and Prime Minister Churchill in Quebec in August, 1943. The proceedings of this and related meetings were top secret. Not even Vice-President Truman had been informed of the project.[7]

Secretary of War Henry L. Stimson, in a memorandum to President Truman dated September 11, 1945, first proposed that the Soviet Union should be approached in an effort to gain an agreement to limit the use of the atomic bomb as an instrument of war and to promote the peaceful use of atomic energy. Before approaching the Russians, however, the Secretary suggested that we should first reach agreement with Britain on the questions to be discussed.

President Truman had received a message from Prime Minister Attlee on August 8, 1945 which suggested that the United States and Great Britain issue a joint statement of our intentions to utilize the existence of this great power

not for our own ends, but as trustees for humanity in the interest of all people in order to promote peace and justice for the world.[8]

The President's reply of August 15 stated that he shared Attlee's views.

The following month, on September 25, the Prime Minister suggested that the United States and Britain hold joint discussions on the future of our atomic partnership. On November 11, President Truman, Prime Minister Attlee and Canadian Prime Minister Mackenzie King met in Washington. From this meeting came the first official proposal to establish a commission within the United Nations to study the problems of atomic energy.

The second official proposal for the creation of a commission to study atomic energy was formulated at the Moscow Conference of Foreign Ministers of the Soviet Union, the United Kingdom, and the United States, in December,

1945. Together with the foreign ministers of France and China, agreement was reached on the terms of a joint resolution to be presented to the General Assembly of the United Nations.[9] The resolution was presented by the delegation of the United Kingdom on behalf of the five permanent members of the Security Council and Canada. On January 24, 1946, at the seventeenth plenary meeting of the General Assembly in London, a resolution was unanimously adopted establishing a commission to deal with the problems raised by the discovery of atomic energy and other related matters.[10] The commission was to be accountable to the Security Council.[11]

Contrary to the expectations of the early advocates of the United Nations, the organization, in its first month of existence, not only considered regulation of armaments, but also dealt with the more formidable problem of atomic disarmament.

The original United States approach to control of atomic energy hoped for cooperation with the Soviet Union in its peaceful uses as well as acceptance of joint controls as a first step measure. This approach soon proved unsatisfactory due to the extremely complicated controls found to be necessary from the Western point of view to insure that future uses of atomic energy would be for peaceful purposes only. In addition, the Congress, on July 30, 1946, passed the McMahon Atomic Energy Act which stifled any exchange of information on atomic energy.[12] Here we have an early example to show that the United States, as well as the Soviet Union, has been responsible for the arms control deadlock. The Act created a governmental monopoly of sources and prohibited private activity in the field of nuclear energy. Close analysis of the Act revealed that the total effect was to show a deep-seated mistrust by the Congress. No type of international arrangement could be entered into without approval of the Senate. The plain intent of this definition was to exclude the possibility of an executive agreement binding the country with respect to atomic energy.[13]

The agreement between East and West, reached at the Moscow Conference in December, 1945,[14] in regard to the creation of the Atomic Energy Commission, did not extend to the area of actual arms control. Elements of disarmament are so entangled with the sensitive political questions that the subject cannot be treated as simply a self-contained problem. Each atomic power is most cautious about any kind of arms control or disarmament which might leave it at a disadvantage.[15] These nuclear powers have attempted to restrict or eliminate the armaments with which their enemies were best supplied, or in which the enemy was most proficient. One's own armaments are always defensive in nature and therefore do not threaten world peace.[16]

On June 14, 1946, the Atomic Energy Commission held its first meeting at Hunter College, New York. The Commission established various committees in order to perform more effectively. A Working Committee, comprised of one representative from each of the nations represented on the Commission, was established to consider all proposals and suggestions made at sessions of the

Commission and to make recommendations.

In a speech to the first meeting of the Atomic Energy Commission on June 14, 1946, Bernard M. Baruch, the United States Representative and Acting President of the Commission, laid before that body his government's proposals for the control of atomic energy. In the technical parts of his statement, Baruch followed closely the Acheson-Lilienthal report, but in the political field of international control of atomic energy, the Baruch proposals strengthened the technical report. Briefly, the Baruch Plan called for: (1) an international control of atomic energy at the source, with an authority exercising complete control over the production and processing of all raw materials; (2) an international licensing system to promote peacetime uses of atomic energy by the leasing of needed materials; (3) the strategic distribution of plants and stockpiles of fissionable materials throughout the world; (4) free access by the International Authority into all countries to conduct inspection and control activities; (5) the fixing of penalties for any violations; and (6) the elimination of the veto power in decisions involving punishment for violation of the atomic agreement.[17]

After a system of effective controls was brought into operation by successive stages, the United States would cease the production of atomic weapons and dispose of its existing stockpile according to terms of the agreement. Security was an all-important element of the Baruch Plan. Gradual disclosure of atomic secrets was to take place only after controls had been thoroughly tested.

Except for the Communist bloc, reaction to the American proposal was overwhelmingly favorable throughout the world and within the United Nations. Outside of the Communist nations, the most criticism was heard within the United States itself. Thomas E. Murry, former member of the United States Atomic Energy Commission, felt that the Baruch Plan was "supremely idealistic and rashly naive." Mr. Murry felt that if the Soviets had accepted the United States proposal, it would have stopped our nuclear weapons program while allowing them to press forward with nuclear weapons by circumventing the inspection systems which could have been established at that time.[18]

Within the United States, there seemed to be little agreement as to the type of deterrent force the nation should possess. This, in turn, caused disagreement over the program in the Atomic Energy Commission of the United Nations. Disagreement was also widespread over the possible effects of a nuclear attack as well as the precautions to be taken against such an incident.

One group believed that no sane nation would attack another that had a sufficient number of nuclear weapons. Under these conditions, the only fear facing the nuclear powers of the world was the fear of insanity, irresponsibility, accident and miscalculation.[19] Believers in this theory felt that the military stature of nations would not affect the decision of another nation to launch an attack.

From this viewpoint, warning systems and other forms of protection were wasted effort. If nuclear war between the United States and the Soviet Union developed, it would automatically result in world annihilation. This approach, as Kahn points out, fails to distinguish between the attacker and the defender.[20] Although such an attack would be a major catastrophe, the extent of death and damage would depend, to a great degree, upon preparations taken against such an attack. Because of the views mentioned, this group believed that only a small nuclear force was needed for deterrence, since war could only start by accident.

Another school of thought at this time believed that United States military policy should rest on an overwhelming nuclear deterrent. Any type of counter-force was a waste of effect which detracted from the so-called "first line" approach.

Both of these extreme approaches fail to take into consideration the possibility of limited wars or, to use the terminology of the Communist bloc, limited wars and wars of national liberation.

These two extremes, and the example cited above,[21] show that there was no consensus of opinion as to the type of deterrent policy which the United States should follow during this period. Because of this, American and Western policy, at times, did not seem to be too concrete.

The American proposal of June 14 showed that, under certain circumstances, the United States would give up its atomic advantage. This, in turn, gave the United States moral freedom to use atomic weapons if no agreement could be reached with the Soviet Union and the Communist Bloc nations. William Frye points out that such proposals strengthened the bomb's value as a deterrent.[22]

Stalin saw little difference between United States control and control by an international agency. Any such international agency would have a majority friendly to the West in its composition. Under these circumstances, the Soviet Union would never be able to obtain atomic know-how legitimately since all legal research would be under United Nations' control.[23]

At the second meeting of the United Nations' Atomic Energy Commission, on June 19, 1946, Soviet delegate Andrei Gromyko presented his government's plan for atomic disarmament. Based upon the fact that the Soviet Union did not have the bomb at this time, the plan called for immediate prohibition of production of all atomic weapons for the purposes of mass destruction.[24] This was to be put forth in the form of a treaty. Under the treaty, the signatories would also agree to: (1) destroy, within three months after ratification of the agreement, all atomic weapons; and (2) to pass legislation, within six months after ratification of the treaty, providing punishment for violation of the agreement. The treaty would be of indefinite duration and open to all nations of the world, whether or not they were members of the United Nations.

Under the Soviet proposal, atomic energy development would be carried out by individual nations rather than by an international authority as called for in the Baruch Plan. Final approval of the Soviet approach would be by the Security Council, and after this approval, the convention would be binding on all states whether members or non-members of the United Nations.[25]

The Russian proposals called merely for an international convention out-lawing the production and use of atomic weapons, and required the destruction of all atomic stockpiles. The Soviets were against any system of international inspection, control and punishment. They refused to consider surrender of the veto, protesting that this did violence to national sovereignty.[26]

After viewing the above material, the major differences between the Soviet and United States plans become obvious. The United States plan proposed, ultimately, to give a monopoly on atomic development to an international agency with authority to conduct inspections to insure that all nations were living up to the terms of the treaty. The Soviet proposal, on the other hand, after renouncing atomic weapons, stated that each nation would make itself responsible for any violations. This does not mean, however, that Russia excluded the establishment of an international inspection system after atomic weapons had been destroyed.

The United States called for a gradual disclosure of information, starting with the least important knowledge and not reaching the final stage of elimination of atomic weapons until an inspection system was in full operation. The Soviet approach, reversing this, called for the immediate outlawing of atomic weapons and the omission of the step-by-step approach.

The Baruch Plan also insisted that whatever the agency responsible for enforcing the atomic agreement, no veto (such as existed in the Security Council) could be allowed to halt punishment of offending nations. The Soviets insisted, just as strongly, on retention of the veto and giving the Security Council the final say on punishment for violations of the agreement.

The step-by-step approach insisted upon by the United States came under heaviest attack by the Soviet Union. The United States was determined not to jeopardize its national security before a system of international control and inspection would be established. The Soviets saw in this the West's determination to keep a monopoly on atomic weaponry for an indefinite period. On the other hand, the Russian plan relied merely on the outlawing of atomic warfare by legislation before an effective system of inspection and control could be established. Nevertheless, the need for some type of on-site inspection remains. This will be shown and discussed in regard to nuclear testing at a later point.

During this period, international control of atomic weapons became the dominant diplomatic issue dividing East and West. If the Soviet Union had accepted the Baruch Plan in the form in which it was presented, she would have been without a national atomic energy program. This would have forced the Soviet Union to remain technologically inferior in the atomic area and would have forced the lifting of the iron curtain as well.

British writer P. M. S. Blackett points out that the leaders of the Soviet Union felt that secrecy of the location of their nuclear bases was an absolute necessity in the face of United States superiority in nuclear weapons.[27] The Soviet demand for full inspection only in the last stage was consistent with the reliance for safety from nuclear attack on small, purely retaliatory weapons in secret locations. International inspection would have served to reveal the locations of Soviet missile sites as well as to show how small the Soviet retaliatory force was at this time.

Today, the Soviet Union has taken certain countermeasures, such as hardening and dispersing its missiles. These changes make it less dependent on secrecy to avoid vulnerability to surprise attack. Detection by radar and satellites has also made it possible to inspect without creating an elaborate apparatus for this purpose by treaty.

The political approach, if it is to be successful, must of necessity be based upon concrete and specific proposals. There are no precedents to serve as guides in this field and the problem is further complicated by the necessity of providing for adequate utilization of atomic energy for peaceful purposes. The achieving of international security would be much simpler if atomic energy had no industrial uses.

On December 30, the Atomic Energy Commission submitted its first report to the Security Council. The report, based essentially on the Baruch Plan, recommended that a comprehensive international system of control and inspection be defined by a treaty, in which all the United Nations would be entitled to participate. It also spelled out what would constitute a violation and the penalities involved. The Commission recognized that it had not yet taken up the problem of how the various safeguards were to be administered as part of the overall system. Also recognized was the fact that the suggested safeguards did not represent a plan for atomic energy control, but rather, some of the elements which should be incorporated into any effective plan.

The report recommended that the treaty include the entire program for putting the system into effect. The Commission was to determine when any particular stage had been completed and the next was to begin.[28]

Ten nations, including the United States and Britain, approved the American Plan in the Atomic Energy Commission. The Soviet Union and Poland abstained in the voting. In the Security Council, the Russian veto blocked approval.

The first serious move by the Soviet Union in the area of international control of atomic energy came in June, 1947, in a proposal presented by Andrei Gromyko. In addition to an international convention prohibiting atomic weapons, a separate treaty was to provide for an International Control Commission to enforce peaceful development of atomic energy. This agency was to be composed of members of the Atomic Energy Commission and was to have an international staff of inspectors who could make periodic checks at reported atomic facilities. The Security Council was to have jurisdiction over violations; therefore, the big power veto was in effect.

Under the provisions of the Soviet proposal, nations could have undertaken unrestricted research into peaceful uses of atomic energy. Prohibition of atomic weapons was to take precedence over the establishment of controls. Whereas the

Baruch Plan had proposed the international ownership and management of atomic materials, the Gromyko proposal suggested that they be left in national hands but made subject to inspection. The inspection system was to be fairly extensive but only on a periodic basis. Control would not become effective until after the United States had destroyed its atomic stockpile.

In September, the United Nations Atomic Energy Commission adopted its second report. The report stated that the Soviet proposals of June 11 did not provide an adequate basis for development of specific plans for effective controls. The Commission's report added a list of proposals concerning the function of an international control agency, which, in effect, followed the recommendations of the United States.[29] The Soviet Union voted against the adoption of the Commission's Second Report to the Security Council.[30]

By September, 1947, the lines in the Atomic Energy Commission were rigidly drawn between the Soviet position and the majority plan which was essentially based on the United States proposals. As mentioned above, the second report was devoted primarily to the differences between the Soviet position and that of the Western members.[31] The minor agreements reached after this time only narrowed the gap on a few specific points.

On June 22, 1948, the Soviet Union vetoed a United States resolution in the Security Council which proposed the adoption of the three reports of the United Nations Atomic Energy Commission. The Council subsequently voted to submit the reports to the General Assembly. This was possible since it was a procedural decision and, therefore, not subject to veto. In November, the Third Regular Session of the General Assembly gave overwhelming endorsement to the first report of the United Nations Atomic Energy Commission, thus, in effect, approving the essentials of the Baruch Plan. The resolution also called on the Commission to resume its work.[32] General Assembly action had little effect on the negotiating process, but it did benefit the West from the moral as well as the propaganda standpoint.

At this point, the Soviet Union slightly modified its previous proposals. Earlier proposals had called for two conventions. The first would prohibit nuclear weapons and the second would establish a system of control. Now the Soviet delegate suggested that the two conventions should go into effect simultaneously. Another suggested alternative was to establish one convention with two parts. It soon became evident that the deadlock was to continue. The Soviet proposal became entangled in an attempt to define the terminology "into force simultaneously." Was this to mean immediately, or was it to mean when the control agencies were completed? The Soviet Union consistently avoided this issue. Discussions broke down in 1949 when it became apparent in the Atomic Energy Commission that the term "control," from the Soviet point of view, meant exactly the same as it had in their proposal of June, 1947. This proposal had already been declared unacceptable by the Western powers.

A General Assembly resolution requested that the Atomic Energy Commission continue consultations. These meetings took place between August and October, 1949. As had been the case from its inception, the Commission was completely unable to develop a plan which could gain unanimous support. The majority of the Commission members came to the conclusion that if the development of atomic energy was to be left in the hands of each government, no form of international supervision could guarantee protection against illicit production. Under these conditions, the Commission recommended that member states relinquish a large measure of sovereignty and create an International Control Agency to see that all activities in the area of atomic energy be carried on

under powers of operation and management and under rights of ownership or by nations under licence from the agency.[33]

The minority plan, which was sponsored by the Soviet Union, placed primary reliance on the voluntary adherence of member states. Supervision of compliance with the rules would be delegated to an international agency operating within the framework of the Security Council. Under this plan there would be conventions drafted on the prohibition of atomic weapons and on the establishment of effective control over atomic energy.[34]

At the first meeting of the permanent members of the Atomic Energy Commission, subsequent to the General Assembly meeting of January 19, 1950, the Soviet Union demanded the seating of the representative of the People's Republic of China. On the rejection of this demand, the Soviet delegation to the Commission, as well as Soviet delegations to all other United Nations organizations, withdrew from participation. This action brought to an end the possibility of any effective action by the Atomic Energy Commission. Problems facing the Commission were not taken up again until after the General Assembly of 1951 abolished the Atomic Energy Commission and the Commission of Conventional Armaments and created the Disarmament Commission to replace them.

The fundamental difference between East and West involved not only methods, but aims as well. Whereas the majority plan put world security first, the minority proposals placed the greatest emphasis upon national sovereignty. Western proposals would have destroyed Soviet secrecy.

Although the Baruch Plan was approved by the majority of Atomic Energy Commission members, it failed to explain in detail when and in what manner the control system would bring about the final elimination of nuclear weapons. It was in this area of inspection and control, however, that the West had its greatest advantage over the Soviet bloc. When failure to reach agreement on the guide lines for an international control agency developed, the blame could easily be placed upon the Russian's unwillingness to permit adequate inspection to guarantee observance of treaty commitments.

On the issue of the veto, the Soviet stand could be more easily justified. Article 24 of the United Nations Charter states that, in order to ensure prompt and effective action by the United Nations, its members confer on the Security Council primary responsibility for the maintenance of international peace and security, and agree that in carrying out its duties under this responsibility, the Security Council acts on their behalf.[35]

Article 26 gives the Security Council the responsibility for

formulating, with the assistance of the Military Staff Committee, plans to be submitted to the Members of the United Nations for the establishment of a system for the regulation of armaments.[36]

Article 27 states that decisions on substantive matters

shall be made by an affirmative vote of seven members including the concurring votes of the permament members . . .[37]

Retention of the veto would provide little protection for the nation who wanted to violate the Charter of the Atomic Development Authority. The use of the veto by a signatory power would be a clear indication of that power's intention to embark upon an atomic weapons development program.

Any disagreement among the great powers that would lead to the call for sanctions would undoubtedly lead to war. As Secretary-General Trygve Lie said in his Annual Report for 1949, "Enforcement action against a great power would not be a police action. It would be war—in fact a new world war."[38]

Commission for Conventional Armaments: Clash of Soviet-American National Security Goals

On February 13, 1947, the Security Council created the Commission for Conventional Armaments. Included in the make-up of this body were the eleven members of the Security Council and Canada. These were the same nations represented on the United Nations Atomic Energy Commission. The Commission was to formulate both general principles and concrete proposals for the reduction of conventional types of national armament. Although the Security Council established the Commission, it was the General Assembly which called for such an organization. Consequently, since the Assembly created the Atomic Energy Commission and was responsible for the creation of the Commission on Conventional Armaments, it had a special interest in the activities of both bodies, even though they reported directly to the Security Council.[39]

During the first year of operation, the Commission for Conventional Armaments accomplished very little, largely because the Commission felt a system for the regulation and reduction of armaments and armed forces could only be put into effect in an atmosphere of international confidence and security. American and Soviet attitudes toward both of the Commissions shifted as advantages swung from one side to the other. As long as the United States had sole possession of atomic weapons, the Soviet Union wished to have both conventional and atomic disarmament considered by one body. When the Soviets developed atomic weapons, they then wanted a separation of the two functions. The attitude of the United States was the reverse of that of the Soviet Union.

As early as October, 1946, four months before the creation of the Commission for Conventional Armaments, Soviet Foreign Minister Molotov introduced a resolution in the General Assembly calling for a reduction of conventional armaments as well as control of atomic energy. The resolution disregarded the Atomic Energy Commission which had already received authorization from the General Assembly to deal with the control of atomic energy. The Soviet Union had previously requested that all members of the United Nations report the number and location of their armed forces in foreign nations.

On March 26, 1947, the Conventional Armaments Commission held its first meeting. The first order of business was to prepare a plan of work.[40] Contrary to the previous decision by the General Assembly, the Soviet Union still tried to include atomic disarmament in the work plan of the Commission. Following the General Assembly session of late 1947, the Conventional Armaments Commission reconvened in 1948. At this time, the Commission adopted, over the opposition of the Soviet Union, the following six principles:

(1) a system for the regulation and reduction of conventional armaments and armed forces should provide for the adherence of all states and initially should include all states having substantial military resources; (2) the system could only be put into effect in an atmosphere of international confidence and security; (3) examples of conditions essential to such confidence and security would be the establishment of an adequate system of agreements under Article 43 of the Charter and the international control of atomic energy; (4) a system for the regulation and reduction of armaments and armed forces should provide for the least possible diversion for armaments of the world's human and economic resources; (5) it must include an adequate system of safeguards which functions under international supervision to insure the observance of the provisions of the treaty or convention; and (6) a provision must be made for effective enforcement action in the event of violations.[41]

As Bechhoefer points out, this stand placed the United States in the position of advocating atomic disarmament without a corresponding improvement in international relations. At the same time, the Western Allies insisted that settlement of political differences was necessary before agreement on conventional disarmament could be reached.[42]

Soviet proposals of 1948 tied atomic weapons and all other armaments together. In September, Andrei Vyshinsky submitted the Soviet proposal to the General Assembly. The same proposal was also introduced in the Conventional Armaments Commission. In addition to calling for the prohibition of atomic weapons and an international control agency under the Security Council, the proposal called for the five permanent members of the Council to reduce their armaments and armed forces by one-third.

The general feeling of the United Nations members, at this time, was that the atomic weapons issue should not be linked, in this way, to conventional armaments. The Western powers rejected the proposal on the grounds of the numerical superiority of Soviet troops. The Soviet proposal, supported only by the Soviet bloc, was voted down by a large majority.

This position by the Western powers was made necessary by the drastic reduction in conventional armaments by the United States and its allies following World War II. Many authorities feel that this was one of the major errors in the immediate postwar policy of the West. It was in the field of conventional high explosive warfare that the United States was most competent. A high technical and economic superiority made this true.

The contention that NATO could not match Russian convential fire power and numbers of ground troops, and therefore would need nuclear weapons to create a balance, did not take into consideration the large, powerfully equipped military machine of the Federal Republic of Germany.

Modern development in the field of conventional armaments seems to favor the status quo powers of the West because their interest is primarily in defense rather than offense.[43]

After eighteen months, the Commission was unable to reach agreement on a set of guiding principles. Confronted with this stalemate, the Assembly, in 1948, endorsed the majority position that disarmament could take place only after an improvement in the atmosphere of international confidence and security.[44]

In the summer of 1948, a change in the policy of the United States began to appear. The first step was the passage of the Vandenberg Resolution by the Senate. This resolution called for a United Nations armed force, as provided by the Charter, an agreement among member nations upon regulation and reduction of armaments and an adequate guarantee against any violations.[45] In the Vandenberg Resolution, the United States was actually repudiating its demand that conventional disarmament, even with adequate safeguards, would not be considered until the Soviet bloc approved the Baruch Plan. The resolution also eliminated the demand by the Western Allies that the settlement of political differences was necessary before agreement on conventional disarmament could be discussed. By moving closer to the Soviet position that both atomic and conventional disarmament problems should be treated as one, the Vandenberg Resolution had the effect of taking the initiative from the Soviet bloc in the United Nations disarmament discussions.

The Third General Assembly in November, 1948, directed the Commission on Conventional Armaments to devote

its first attention to formulating proposals for the receipt, checking and publication, by an international organ of control within the framework of the Security Council, of full information to be supplied by member states with regard to their effectives and their conventional armaments.[46]

In keeping with the Assembly directive, the French Government prepared a plan for a census and verification of the armed forces of all United Nations members. This was a comprehensive plan which called for a breakdown of the military census into types of military units, including description of each plus a description of the reserve units of each nation. The census would also cover the number of automatic weapons and artillery, classified by type and caliber, armor, combatant ships and aircraft, classified by type, and the total quantity of material, both in service and in reserve. Data regarding research and experimental material was specifically excluded from the census.

In dealing with the control of forces in existence, many technical problems arose. What factors of military strength shall be dealt with and in what order? How can these factors be combined so as to permit comparison between the strength of different states.[47] As can be seen, an attempt to deal with the whole range of military forces becomes much more difficult because of the technical complexities. In measuring relative power, many factors have to be considered. For the above reasons, a first-step, partial-measures approach seems to be the only possibility for achieving eventual agreements in the area of disarmament.

The plan further provided that the census was to be carried out and verified by a Central Control Authority which would be granted freedom of movement and access to data needed. Decisions of the Authority would be adopted by a simple majority, but its parent body, the Control Organ, would be directly subordinate to the Security Council.[48]

The Soviet Union objected to the French plan. Before any such plan could become effective, the Soviets insisted that an agreement for the reduction of conventional armaments and armed forces, plus the prohibition of atomic weapons, must be reached.

On August 1, 1949, the Commission on Conventional Armaments approved the French Plan over Soviet objections. The report of the Commission to the Security Council was vetoed on October 18. In December, the General Assembly approved the report of the Commission—embodying the French Plan for conventional disarmament. As was the case in the General Assembly's approval of the reports of the Atomic Energy Commission, the Assembly's approval of the Commission on Conventional Armaments report was of little value. Without great power agreement, progress in the field of disarmament was impossible.

Following the meeting of the Fourth General Assembly in 1949, the Conventional Armaments Commission did not resume its session until April 27, 1950. At that time, the Soviet representative walked out of the meeting following the Commission's refusal of his request to seat the representative of Communist China. Even though the Soviet Union was not represented, the Commission held several meetings at which the United States introduced three working papers. The Working Committee submitted its report, with the United

States' plan incorporated in it, to the Commission on Conventional Armaments. With the Korean War in progress, plus the absence of the Soviet Union from the Commission, there was no chance for decisive action. The Committee's discussions could be little more than academic under the conditions.

Until late 1950, the Western majority claimed that atomic energy was a special problem to be dealt with separately from conventional armaments. The Soviet bloc maintained that the two questions were linked and that it was impossible to separate them. As early as October, 1950, President Truman, in an address to the General Assembly on United Nations Day, suggested that the Atomic Energy Commission and the Commission for Conventional Armaments of the United Nations might be combined and a new approach made toward breaking the existing deadlock. The President laid down three conditions which he felt must be met in any effective plan for disarmament. Such a plan must include all types of weapons, receive unanimous support and be foolproof.[49]

President Truman's speech represented two major changes in the Western approach. In the first place, the United States recognized that any arms control plan must be based on unanimous agreement. Secondly, it was recognized that any disarmament plan must include all types of weapons. Progress toward reduction of conventional armaments and armed forces was no longer dependent on prior agreement on the international control of atomic energy.

On December 13, 1950, the General Assembly established a Committee of Twelve, consisting of the members of the Security Council plus Canada, to develop a plan for merging the Atomic Energy Commission and the Commission for Conventional Armaments. The resolution was adopted by a majority of forty-seven votes.[50]

The Soviet Union, which had returned to the United Nations, voted against establishing the Committee. Although accusing the West of maneuvering to put the pressing question of the prohibition of atomic weapons and the creation of a control system into "cold storage,"[51] the Soviet and its satellites participated in the work of the Committee of Twelve which, in 1951, issued its report recommending the establishment of the United Nations Disarmament Commission.[52]

In January 1952, the General Assembly established a Disarmament Commission under the Security Council. The Commission was directed to prepare a draft treaty for the regulation, limitation and balanced reduction of all armed forces and armaments, and for the effective international control of atomic energy. The Soviet Union agreed to the formation of the Disarmament Committee but objected to its mandate being based on the Western position. Because of this, the Soviet Union voted against establishing the Disarmament Commission.

Until that time, when international political relations permitted genuine agreement on a plan for the control and reduction of armaments, the new commission could only keep the problem under review and hope that someday agreement would be reached on the major obstacles which stood in the path of disarmament.

General and Complete Disarmament

As early as 1952, the United Nations began a series of meetings in an effort to reach agreement on a formula for general and complete disarmament. No serious discussions were held, however, before the 1955 meetings in London. These international conferences oscillated between attempts at comprehensive arms limitations and rather limited measures. In 1962, the eighteen nation Committee on Disarmament received plans from both the Soviet Union and the United States for a treaty on general and complete disarmament.[53] Each proposal called for: (1) complete conventional and nuclear disarmament in three stages; (2) the establishment of peace-keeping machinery for the disarmed world; and (3) the creation of an International Disarmament Organization (IDO) to implement disarmament controls. Even though the similarities are apparent, beneath these were radically different approaches for each stage of the disarmament process.

Neither plan provided for the transition from one stage to the next in an automatic manner; however, the United States plan was more precautionary. Stage II would begin only after all militarily significant states had adhered to the treaty, and the initiation of stage III would be conditioned upon the adherence of all states possessing armed forces and armaments. The transition to either stage would take place only if the IDO Council, composed of the major powers as permanent members, should declare, by a two-thirds majority including the concurring votes of the Soviet Union and the United States, that the previous stage had been carried out and that preparations for the next stage had been completed.

Both states have added amendments to their original proposals which were put forth in the early 1950's. The Soviet Union seems to have made the most significant change by accepting, at least in principle, the Western demand for the retention of an effective nuclear deterrent throughout the arms control and disarmament process. Foreign Minister Andrei Gromyko agreed that the United States and the Soviet Union could retain a limited number of intercontinental ballistic missiles "in their own territory" until the end of Stage III.[54] The first Gromyko proposal, which was put forth a year earlier, had called for the retention of "a strictly limited and agreed" number of missiles until the end of stage II.[55] Originally, the Soviet Union had proposed the total elimination of all missiles in stage I.

Obviously, neither plan was wholly acceptable to both sides. The United States accused the Soviet Union of "overloading" stage I, thus rendering the Western alliance structures and nuclear deterrent impotent while at the same time leaving the Soviet conventional superiority in Eastern Europe intact. The Soviet Union saw, in the proposal by the United States, a threat to its security if Western military strength was allowed to remain intact during the early stages of disarmament. Today, the Western stipulation that the IDO control power should extend to armaments that remained in the arsenal of world states, as well as to those to be destroyed, continues to provoke strong Soviet denunciation as "legalized espionage" and also unwarranted control over armaments prior to actual disarmament.

The Soviet Union still refuses to discuss elimination of nuclear delivery vehicles until the West accepts the Gromyko proposal, at least in principle. The United States and other Western powers respond that the Soviet Union has not explained what categories and numbers of missiles are to be retained. Other complaints of the West are: (1) that the Soviet proposals could radically shift the military balance; and (2) that the proposals contained inadequate provision for verification.[56]

Any arguments put forth either in favor or against general and complete disarmament can only be hypothetical in nature, since at no time has such an agreement been reached among the world's nation-states. National governments will continue to be guided in their policies by what they consider to be their vital national interests. Different proposals and agreements directed toward arms reduction will be ruled by these same principles. This will continue to be true unless the process of arms control and disarmament should bring the nation-states to merge with one another and to transfer the responsibility for peace-keeping to a supranational force or authority.[57] The probability of this taking place in today's world is no more likely than in past periods of history. Direct relationship between armaments and the vital national interests of the nations still determine the level of armaments maintained by these nations.

In the Soviet plan, peace and security depend simply on the absence of armed forces. Under the Western plan, however, peace and security depend on an international military force. No matter what type of proposal or plan is being discussed, the capacity of states to employ armed coercion or the threat of armed coercion against other states cannot be abolished entirely; therefore, problems of military security will not be eliminated.[58] States would, however, have to deal with these problems in a radically different military environment. The ability of states to employ military power to meet the changing circumstances without violating the disarmament treaty would be severely limited.

Another problem faced in any drastic disarmament approach is the balancing of reductions on each side. At no stage should one side have the advantage; however, throughout history, states have disagreed upon the precise reductions and limitations to be enacted. As mentioned before, because of the constantly changing circumstances, nations are reluctant to jeopardize their vital national interests. Technological innovations, in today's world, might be destructive of this existing stability. Weapons which are conceived in one political period may not be in production until the world has moved on to the next political period. These weapons may create the very conditions that they were originally designed to offset.[59]

A nation's geographic location will play a major part in any disarming world.

It would seem, as Robert Osgood points out, that disarmament would enhance the protection of states from attack in proportion to their remoteness from their adversaries.[60] This would eliminate most long-range weapons as well as reduce troops available for invasion purposes and the means for transporting these troops. States that have common borders, however, would have comparatively easy military access to each other even with their smaller internal security forces.

The resulting imbalances of power among states with conflicting interests would create more insecurity and tension among these states than a world without such an agreement. Major industrial powers could develop an over-powering strike within a few months. In the absence of an effective peacekeeping force, general and complete disarmament would create a greater imbalance of power as well as new reasons for states to war upon each other. If a stable world order did emerge, it would probably be because of the development of a new system of alliances.[61]

Another program, advocated by some as a solution to the arms control and disarmament problem, is the unilateral approach. In the broad sense, this would entail the unconditional dismantling of the state's military establishment. This type of arms control will be accepted by neither the Western powers nor the Soviet Union. Rather than leading to a world free from wars, measures that drastically change the existing distribution of military power would more likely bring new territorial conflicts to the surface.[62]

A form of unilateral disarmament somtimes called "graduated unilateral action," calls for the United States to gradually take steps toward disarmament in hopes that the Soviet Union would reciprocate.[63] It would be hoped that by inducing the Soviet to reciprocate, a break in the arms control deadlock would develop. From the military standpoint, this would be clearly disadvantageous to the side making the concession, but these should be small enough so that failure by the other side to make an equal concession would not be crippling.

Any such unilateral move should be of a nature that reciprocal action by the enemy is clearly available. It should also be announced in advance and widely publicized but the act should not demand a prior commitment from the other side.[64]

The more comprehensive the provisions of a disarmament treaty are, the more violations and the more unstable that treaty will be; however, every violation should not necessarily terminate the entire agreement. Minor violations are bound to occur when an agreement or treaty applies many restrictions to the armed forces and war potential of so many states.

The possibility of an international agreement on an all-embracing reduction and limitation of armaments is very small indeed. Such an agreement on the level at which armaments are to be frozen once again involves the problem of ratio, an approach which has never worked in the past. Limited or partial measures are more consistent with the retention by the nation-states of some control over the type and level of their armament. General and complete disarmament requires universal agreement in areas in which the nations of the world are most divided. Most measures of this type have required agreement on prior stages or levels before proceeding to the next stage. These approaches are, in reality, limited or partial arms control measures rather than the general and complete approach.

Evaluation of the Period

During the early years of the United Nations, arms control and disarmament negotiations followed the pattern of political events. Whenever political differences narrowed, a corresponding narrowing of the differences in arms control talks was noted. From this, it becomes evident that world affairs outside the area of arms control—in other words, political questions—were far more important than those dealing solely with disarmament.

Early United Nations efforts at arms control and disarmament were stifled by the same underlying causes that still exist today. The first of these, the relationship of any arms control agreement to the inspection and control system established to insure compliance with the treaty, has been the principle factor in the failure of negotiations. Involved here is the issue of secrecy versus information. This has taken the form of disputes over the level and type of inspection needed in both specific arms control measures and in the various stages of a general and complete disarmament agreement. The Soviet Union alleges that the United States wants a large amount of inspection without much arms control, while at the same time, the United States contends that the Soviet Union cannot be serious about arms control measures unless it is willing to support machinery for its effective enforcement. In both the Atomic Energy Commission and the Commission for Conventional Armaments, the Soviet Union insisted upon two separate treaties. The first would provide for the elimination of nuclear weapons. In the Commission for Conventional Armaments, a blanket one-third cut in all forces and equipment was proposed. The second treaty, which was not to become effective until after the first treaty was approved and in operation, would establish a system of safeguards. To the United States and the other Western nations, the Soviet demand was totally unacceptable; however, under existing world conditions Western proposals to reverse the order in which the two treaties would become operative were just as unacceptable to the Soviets.

Contrary to the central theme of many books and articles written in the United States on the topic of arms control and disarmament, world conditions at this time, as far as the Eastern Bloc nations were concerned, justified the Soviet stand. Without access to atomic weapons, it was only natural that the Soviet Union would strive to promote her national security by demanding that destruction of nuclear weapons must be the first step in any disarmament program. The fact that the Western proposals, at a later date, suggested that both treaties become effective simultaneously showed that its proposals, in this period, were as far out of line as were those put forth by the Soviet Union. When this approach was rejected by the East, the Western position was much more acceptable to world opinion than was that of the Soviet Union. By showing a willingness to compromise on points of disagreement, the Western powers were able, at this time, to place the blame for lack of agreement on the arms control question at the door of the Soviet bloc.

The second major stumbling block in the path of agreement on arms control measures was soon found to be the relationship of arms limitation to political settlement. In the Atomic Energy Commission of the United Nations, the United States took the position that international control of atomic energy should take place, regardless of the progress toward settlement of political questions. Several months later, in the Commission for Conventional Armament, the United States' position was not only that reduction of Conventional Armaments could not take place without a corresponding improvement of political differences, but also that discussions of such reductions could not proceed until an agreement was reached on these political differences. The Soviet Union simply evaded the issue, and from that time used the Commission as a platform for propaganda purposes.

While offering to abandon atomic weapons, in which the United States was far superior to the Soviet Union, the West, at the same time, was rejecting efforts to reduce conventional forces. Because of the drastic reductions of armed forces and equipment following World War II, any further cut in these forces would have increased the advantage of the Soviet Union in this area. This, in all probability, was the main reason for the failure of the Baruch Plan to explain in detail the type of inspection system which must be in operation before the United States would destroy its nuclear stockpile.

Once again, the United States' position, both in the Atomic Energy Commission and in the Commission for Conventional Armaments, left much to be desired. Lack of coordination among the delegates dealing with the arms control and disarmament problem was one of the major short-comings of the United States approach. Whereas the representative on the Military Staff Committee received his instructions directly from the Joint Chiefs of Staff, the Department of State was responsible for formulating not only over-all foreign policy, but also arms control negotiations policy. Mr. Baruch's stature was such that, with direct access to the president, he was, to a certain degree, free to formulate policy within the Atomic Energy Commission without being subordinate to officials of the State Department. This type of split responsibility might work reasonably well in the short run. In the long run, however, this is not true.

The Soviet Union had no problem in coordinating its policy on armament negotiations. Unlike the United States, any change in administration or policy simply meant that Soviet representatives changed their approach to correspond to the new policy. Such men as Gromyko, Sobolev, Zorin, Tsarapkin and Malik have been associated with Soviet foreign policy and, in particular, with arms control and disarmament negotiations since the end of World War II.

By 1950, the United States and the Western Powers were beginning to recognize that arms control agreements, if they were to be effective, required the backing of all the great powers. At the same time, the United States changed its approach in the area of weapons control. The demand that a plan for the control of atomic energy be accepted prior to any plan for the reduction of conventional armaments was dropped. Now, as mentioned previously, the United States advocated the combining of the two areas of disarmament. With the change in the political situation, the Soviet Union, now having nuclear weapons, found it to her advantage to demand that disarmament negotiations be carried on separately in areas of atomic and conventional weapons.

In the following chapter, which deals with specific areas of arms control and disarmament, it will be noted that most of the problems which have been discussed in the preceding chapters, and which have, thus far, resulted in lack of agreement, still remain unsettled today. When examining such topics as nuclear testing, inspection and verification, and nuclear proliferation, we find that some first phase measures have been agreed upon. These, however, are no more than a step in the right direction. Because of the major political differences that separate East and West, it would seem that the only productive approach toward an arms control agreement must continue to be the slow, methodical, step by step agreements which we hope will lead toward the final goal of arms control with verification.

FOOTNOTES

[1] Clark M. Eichelberger, *The United Nations: The First Fifteen Years* (New York: Harper and Brothers, 1960), p. 42.

[2] Bernard G. Bechhoefer, *Postwar Negotiations for Arms Control*, Washington, D.C.: The Brookings Institute, 1961, pp. 31–32.

[3] Eichelberger, p. 40.

[4] *Ibid.*

[5] Bernard G. Bechhoefer, *Postwar Negotiations for Arms Control*, p. 14. Also see the *Treaty for the Prevention of War*, League of Nations, *Treaty Series*, Vol. 94, pp. 57–64.

[6] *The Charter of the United Nations and the Statute of the International Court of Justice*, pp. 23–24.

[7] Harry S. Truman, *Memoirs by Harry S. Truman, Vol. I: Year of Decisions*, New York: Doubleday and Company, 1955, pp. 10–11.

[8] *Ibid.*, p. 523.

[9] James F. Byrnes, *Speaking Frankly*, New York: Harper and Brothers, 1947, pp. 266–269.

[10] United Nations, Department of Public Information, *The Control of Atomic Energy*, pp. 1–2.

[11] *United Nations, General Assembly, Official Records:* First Session, Part I, 17th Plenary Meeting, 24 January, 1946, p. 267.

[12] James R. Newman and Byron S. Miller, *The Control of Atomic Energy: A Study of Its Social, Economic, and Political Implications*, (New York: McGraw-Hill Book Company, 1948), pp. 3–4.

[13] *Ibid.*, pp. 265–266.

[14] *Supra*, p. 84.

[15]Harold Courlander, *Shaping Our Times: What the United Nations Is and Does,* (New York: Oceana Publications, Inc., 1960), pp. 159–160.

[16]William R. Frye, "Characteristics of Recent Arms-Control Proposals and Agreements," *Daedalus,* LXXXIX, Fall, 1960, p. 725.

[17]See *Official Records of Atomic Energy Commission,* first meeting, 14 June 1946, pp. 10–13.

[18]Thomas E. Murry, *Nuclear Policy for War and Peace,* New York: World Publishing Co., 1960, p. 72.

[19]Herman Kahn, *On Thermonuclear War,* Princeton, New Jersey: Princeton University Press, 1960, p. 8.

[20]*Ibid.,* p. 9.

[21]*Supra,* p. 90.

[22]Frye, p. 726.

[23]*Ibid.*

[24]Robert E. Riggs, *Illinois Studies in the Social Sciences,* Vol. XLI: *Politics in the United Nations: A Study of United States Influence in the General Assembly,* Urbana: University of Illinois Press, 1958, p. 109.

[25]*Official Records of Atomic Energy Commission:* first year, 1946, pp. 26–28.

[26]Bernard M. Baruch, *The Public Years,* New York: Holt, Rinehart and Winston, 1960, p. 372.

[27]P. M. S. Blackett, "Steps Toward Disarmament," *Strategy of World Order,* ed. Richard A. Falk and Saul H. Mendlovitz, New York: World Law Fund, 1966, p. 20.

[28]Byrnes, p. 386.

For complete text of report see *Official Records of Atomic Energy Commission,* First Year, Special Supplement, 31 December, 1946.

[29]For complete text of the Second Report of the Atomic Energy Commission to the Security Council, see, *Official Records of Atomic Energy Commission,* second year, Special Supplement, 11 September, 1947.

[30]For Gromyko reply, see *Official Records of the Atomic Energy Commission,* second year, 10 September, 1947, pp. 41–53.

[31]Bechhoefer, p. 54.

[32]See United Nations Document No. AEC/C.1/77/Rev.1.

[33]*Official Record of the Atomic Energy Commission,* third year, Special Supplement, (Doc. A.E.C./31), 25 May 1948, p. 17.

[34]*Annual Report of the Secretary-General on the Work of the Organization, 1 July 1948 – 30 June 1949,* Document Supplement Number 1 (A/930), p. 47.

[35]*Charter of the United Nations and Statute of the International Court of Justice,* p. 15.

[36]*Ibid.,* p. 16.

[37]*Ibid.,* p. 17. With the increase of Security Council membership from eleven to fifteen, an affirmative vote of nine members is needed.

[38]*Annual Report of the Secretary-General on the Work of the Organization, 1 July 1948 – 30 June 1949,* Doc. Supplement No. 1 (A/930), p. XII.

[39]"The United Nations General Assembly: Its Expanding Role and the Issues before the Second Session," *International Conciliation,* No. 433, September, 1947, p. 486.

[40]United Nations Commission on Conventional Armaments, Doc. S/C.3/SR.1(26 March, 1947), p. 5.

[41]Bechhoefer, pp. 88–89.

[42]*Ibid.*, p.

[43]Herman Kahn, *On Escalation: Metaphors and Scenarios,* New York: Praeger, 1965, p. 107.

[44]First Progress Report of the Working Committee of the Commission for Conventional Armaments, 20 August 1947 – 2 August 1948, Doc. S/C.3/27, 4 August 1948, p. 7.

[45]For the complete text of the Vandenberg Resolution see U. S. Congress, Senate, 80th Congress, 2nd Session, S. Res. 239, 11 June, 1948.

[46]*Official Records of the General Assembly,* Third Session, Part. I, Resolution 192 (III), December 1948, p. 18.

[47]Tarr, Jr., Cedric W., "Conventional Weapons Control," *Current History,* XLVII (July, 1964), p. 27.

[48]See U. N. Doc. S/C.3/40, 20 July 1949, pp. 3–6.

[49]*Official Records of the General Assembly,* Fifth Session, 295th Plenary Meeting, 24 October, 1950, p. 247.

[50]See General Assembly Resolution 496 (V), 13 December, 1950.

[51]*Official Records of the General Assembly,* Fifth Session, 321st. Plenary Meeting, 12 December 1950, p. 612.

[52]*Official Records of the General Assembly,* Sixth Session, Annexes, "Report of the Committee of Twelve," (23 October, 1951), pp. 2–3.

[53]ENDC/2/Rev.1, 26 November, 1962 and ENDC/30, 18 April, 1962.

[54]U. N. Doc. A/Pv.1208, 19 September, 1963.

[55]GAOR: 17th Sess., 1127th Plenary Meeting, 21 September, 1962.

[56]ENDC/Pv.175, 17 March, 1964, pp. 6–9.

[57]Arnold Wolfers, *The United States in a Disarmed World,* (Baltimore: John Hopkins Press, 1966), p. 4.

[58]Robert E. Osgood, "Military Power in a Disarming and Disarmed World," *The United States in a Disarmed World,* ed. Arnold Wolfers (Baltimore: John Hopkins Press, 1966), p. 38.

[59]Alstair Buchan, "Instabilities of Stalemates," *Current,* (September, 1963), pp. 22–23.

[60]Robert E. Osgood, p. 39.

[61]*Ibid.*, p. 43.

[62]Wolfers, p. 11.

[63]Erich Fromm, "The Case for Unilateral Disarmament," *Arms Control, Disarmament and National Security,* ed. Donald G. Brennan (New York: George Brazilier, 1961), p. 187.

[64]*Ibid.*

CHAPTER IV
THE PARTIAL NUCLEAR TEST
BAN TREATY: AN EXAMPLE
OF LIMITED SUCCESS

Since the end of World War II, disarmament negotiations have been going on continuously. Sometimes these were held within the framework of the United Nations; however, in recent years, such discussions have been held outside of the world peace organization. Even so, the United Nations continues to play a major role in the area of disarmament. Any new developments are thoroughly examined, especially in the following session of the General Assembly.

From these negotiations there have emerged a few steps in the direction of arms control.[1] The first of these was the agreement between the United States and the Soviet Union on a direct communications link between Washington and Moscow, which was signed June 20, 1963.[2] The next agreement, and the only formal treaty on arms control thus far, was the treaty banning nuclear weapon tests in the atmosphere, in outer space, and under water. This treaty was signed by the United States, the United Kingdom and the Soviet Union on August 5, 1963.[3] Following the Moscow signing, the Senate of the United States gave its approval on September 24, 1963.[4] President Kennedy's signature was attached on October 7, 1963. Since this date, over a hundred nations have signed the partial test-ban treaty.

Although the agreement bans all but underground tests, it does not end the threat of nuclear war. Nuclear stockpiles are not reduced, nor is the production of nuclear weapons halted.

Early Test-Ban Controversy

The nuclear weapon tests controversy began shortly after the end of the Second World War. As early as the summer of 1946, following the Bikini Atoll tests, the Military Order of the Purple Heart came out strongly against such tests. This was the signal for many other groups to join in the protest against the harmful effects of nuclear testings. In 1952, Dr. Vannevar Bush, chief scientific adviser to President Truman in the weapons field, suggested to Secretary of State Dean Acheson that the United States and the Soviet Union reach an agreement not to test hydrogen bombs. So far as is known, Dr. Bush was the first to advance formally the idea of a hydrogen bomb test-ban.[5]

The urgent nature of the problem was reflected in the April 19th decision of the Disarmament Commission to create a sub-committee, consisting of the United Kingdom, the United States and the Soviet Union. By this device, the three nuclear powers of the period were brought together. From this beginning, it was hoped that agreement, at least as to a starting point for arms control talks, could be reached. Any optimism in this area soon proved to be groundless. Soviet Ambassador Semyom Tsarapkin introduced a resolution in the United Nations Trusteeship Council charging that the United States had violated its trust by holding nuclear-weapons tests in the Marshall Islands. Included in the resolution was one of the Soviet Union's first official calls to end all nuclear testing.[6]

Without any advance warning, on May 10, 1955, Jacob Malik, the Soviet delegate to the Disarmament Commission's Subcommittee, introduced a completely new proposal which went far beyond any previous Soviet suggestions. For the first time, the Soviet dealt with nuclear tests, proposing their discontinuance under the supervision of an international commission. At the time, the plan was regarded as a genuinely new and serious approach, the first which Moscow had ever made in the arms field.[7] In a key address to the Twentieth Communist Party Congress in February, 1956, Nikita Khrushchev further emphasized the Soviet decision to make a major effort to secure agreement among the great powers on partial arms control measures. The Khrushchev speech continued to call for the early dismantling of all United States overseas bases, a provision which was clearly unacceptable to the West. The Soviet leader had once again attached impossible conditions to his proposal. Western leaders, including President Eisenhower, saw nothing to gain by a test-ban which was not part of a larger disarmament program. From the Western point of view, control of nuclear weapons, rather than their elimination, should be the approach taken. Inspection along with production, rather than testing, was the chief problem.[8]

Subcommittee of the United Nations Disarmament Commission

The United States did not take public notice of the test-ban until 1956. At the Disarmament Subcommittee meetings in London, Mr. Stassen called for limitation of nuclear tests rather then their elimination. The test-ban remained only one part of the overall problem in the Western approach. A plan, proposed by the United Kingdom and France at London on March 19, included the reduction of nuclear tests in the second stage of a comprehensive disarmament program, to be followed by a ban on nuclear tests for military purposes. A follow-up proposal by the United States insisted that nuclear tests must be limited, but more important, before any drastic limitation could take place, a fool-proof inspection system must be created and in operation.

By July, the Soviet government was claiming that the termination of tests would be self-policing. Mr. Dimitri Shepilov, the Soviet representative, stated before the Disarmament Commission that scientific means existed to detect all nuclear tests conducted anywhere in the world—a statement which drew a quick denial from the White House.

During these early years of the nuclear-testing controversy, the Soviet Union had seized the issue, which was first brought to the foreground by India's Prime Minister Nehru, and continued to use it as a propaganda tool. At the same time the Western powers tried to avoid frontal opposition by linking the test ban, first, to a complete package including a cut-off of nuclear weapons manufacture as well as the stockpiling of nuclear materials, and then to the cut-off alone. Only later, when the United States had completed its highest priority testing and Britain had become a nuclear power, did the West trade away the link to the cut-off for corresponding Soviet concessions at the three-power test-ban conference in Geneva.

New United States proposals were ready by November, 1956, but were not made public until January 14, 1957. These were introduced in the United Nations Disarmament Subcommittee on March 19, 1957. On the subject of the production of fissionable materials, an early agreement was called for in cutting off their manufacture under effective control. All future production of fissionable materials would be used only for nonweapons purposes under strict international supervision. Following this step, it would then be possible to limit and eventually to eliminate all nuclear testing. At the same time, the United States offered to devote outer space to peaceful uses and called for a cession of nuclear testing in this environment.[9] Vassily V. Kuznetsov, Soviet Deputy Foreign Minister, rejected the outer space proposal. Since the Soviet Union had no bases near enough to the United States to make medium range missiles effective, it had to rely upon intercontinental missiles to keep the East-West strategic balance from being upset.[10] When the 1957 session of the Disarmament Commission's Subcommittee opened in London, the United States moved toward discussion of partial disarmament measures. At the same time the Soviet was reverting to the advocation of comprehensive disarmament proposals. This, however, did not keep the subject of nuclear test suspension from being considered separately.[11]

On June 14th, Valeria Zorin, the Soviet delegate, made a major concession by including a provision for international supervision in a proposal for a two or three year moratorium on nuclear tests. Under this proposal an international agency would check observance of the test-ban through monitoring posts in the Soviet Union, the United Kingdom, the United States, and the Pacific area.[12] The Zorin proposal prompted an optimistic statement from Mr. Stassen to the effect that for the first time in eleven years there seemed to be a possibility for agreement.[13]

In reply, the United States formally suggested a ten month trial suspension of nuclear testing, if the Soviet Union would agree to halt the manufacture of nuclear weapons one month after installation of an international inspection system. The details of the system would be worked out during the ten month trial suspension. For the first time, the United States had agreed that suspension of tests could become effective prior to the installation of control posts. This Western position was unsatisfactory from the Soviet viewpoint. Nuclear weapons production would be considered only on the basis of a prior renunciation of their use by the United States. Since nuclear weapons formed the basis of the Western deterrent, this proposal was rejected.

Next in line for Soviet criticism was the ten month suspension called for by the West. Zorin did, however, indicate a willingness to negotiate the time limit, but mentioned that it must be long enough to affect the next series of United States tests. In August, 1957, Stassen proposed to the Subcommittee meeting that a twelve month suspension of nuclear testing be agreed upon, which would be followed by a second twelve month suspension provided that advances were being made in the area of inspection and control. The West's agreement on a possible test-ban was still carefully hedged. At the same time, the Soviet Union was losing interest and was in the process of preparing for a series of ballistic missile tests.

The above Soviet proposals were introduced at the Twelfth Session of the General Assembly in September, 1957. If, after the two or three year test suspension which was called for in the proposals, there was still no agreement, the whole area of nuclear testing would be reconsidered.[14] Under this approach, the Soviets were actually achieving a test-ban without an inspection guarantee for a two or three year period. This is another example of the Soviet feeling that one concession on the part of the West would bring about others if they waited long enough.

With a deadlock reached by November, Prime Minister Nehru once again appealed to the United States and the Soviet Union to stop all nuclear explosions.[15] In reply to the Prime Minister, President Eisenhower stated that the United States was prepared to stop nuclear tests immediately, but that this step could not be isolated from other measures which went to the heart of the problem. The United States had once again tied the test-ban and the cut-off together.

On December 10, 1957, Premier Bulganin wrote the first of a long series of letters dealing with major world problems to President Eisenhower. One of the issues discussed by the Premier was nuclear test suspension. Bulganin suggested that such a suspension, even if for only two or three years, might lead to better understanding of the arms control problem.

Prior to the fifteen megaton explosion set off by the United States in March, 1954, no important talks had taken place involving the nuclear test-ban. Serious talks were not started until 1957 at the London Subcommittee meetings. Noticeable success, however, did not appear until early 1958.[16] Soviet rejection of a proposal in the twelfth General Assembly Session to enlarge the Disarmament Commission from eleven to twenty-five members had led to the failure of this body at this time. From this point on, the Soviet Union refused to participate in the Disarmament Commission or its Subcommittee.

Disagreement Within the Scientific Community

At a press conference on March 26, 1958, President Eisenhower mentioned that the United States might be willing to negotiate an agreement for a test cessation without insisting on a cut-off in production of fissionable material for the manufacture of weapons.[17] This shift in attitude was partly due to the studies being conducted by United States scientists on effective means of detecting undisclosed nuclear test explosions. One precondition to any agreement was the assurance that current scientific equipment would be capable of detecting the smallest nuclear explosions. As part of its detection studies, the United States Atomic Energy Commission exploded a seventeen kiloton bomb in an underground shaft in Nevada. This explosion was detected in Alaska, a distance of over 2300 miles.

Arguments Against Test-Ban

The Nevada test did not convince critics of a test-ban treaty. Dr. Edward Teller warned the Senate Disarmament Subcommittee of the difficulties that on-site inspections would have proving that an underground test had taken place. The only way to check would be to bore in and find the radioactivity. This would entail the sending of a large number of inspectors into the Soviet Union.[18] Even then, it would be most difficult, if not impossible, to find the exact spot of the explosion, since radioactivity would only spread a few hundred feet underground.

Admiral Strauss, Chairman of the Atomic Energy Commission, used two arguments against the nuclear test-ban. The test ban would lead to public complacency. This feeling would be manifested in a belief that the need for a large defense effort was no longer needed. The Admiral also felt that not being able to test new weapons would put the United States at a tremendous disadvantage.[19]

Lieutenant General Leslie R. Groves, former head of the Manhattan Project, in testimony before the Senate Disarmament Subcommittee, agreed with those who felt that there was no assurance that all nuclear tests could be detected at this time.[20]

Brigadier General Alfred D. Starbird, Director of Military Application, United States Atomic Energy Commission, reflected the current military feeling on the test-ban in his appearance before the Humphrey Disarmament Subcommittee in March, 1958. The general stated that each warhead design must be tested if it was to be relied on in case of emergency.[21]

Arguments Favoring Test-Ban

Taking the opposite point of view before the Senate Subcommittee was Harrison Brown, Professor of Geochemistry, California Institute of Technology. Dr. Brown believed that an initial agreement would be politically and technologically feasible. First, an agreement to suspend tests for a period long enough for an international panel of scientists, representing the various areas of knowledge involved, to work out specifications for a worldwide network of detection stations, would be needed. Dr. Brown's estimate of the time needed was from one to three years. Next, all tests that could be detected and identified by the system would be banned. These would include underground tests above the one kiloton range. The size of the tests was not the important aspect of the Brown proposal. Elimination of the larger tests was the primary goal. Dr. Brown did not advocate the banning of all nuclear weapons tests for the simple reason that a much more elaborate system would be required to monitor the very small explosions. An agreement such as this would not change the fact that both the Soviet Union and the United States had vast stockpiles of nuclear weapons. Such an agreement would, however, keep the problems from growing worse.[22]

First Test Cessation

On March 31, 1958 the Soviet Union became the first nation to announce a unilateral cessation of nuclear testing. The decree, issued by the Supreme Soviet, declared that if other powers continued to test atomic and hydrogen weapons, the Soviet Union would "act freely in the question of testing."[23] This action, by the Supreme Soviet, created great pressure on the Western powers for a cessation agreement. Most of the world's nations failed to take into consideration that the Soviet government had just completed an intensive series of nuclear tests, while the United States tests were not scheduled to begin until the spring and summer of 1958. Premier Khrushchev informed President Eisenhower of the decree and suggested that the United States and the United Kingdom follow the Soviet lead. The President's reply of April 8th called upon Khrushchev to agree to a conference of technicians, as he had first suggested in January, to study specific control measures for a dependable arms control program. Eisenhower again stressed the need for a cut-off of production of fissionable fuels for military purposes.[24] When the Soviet Premier showed little interest in this proposal, President Eisenhower suggested that the technical talks could be limited to the detection of nuclear tests. The Soviet leader's acceptance of the United States' suggestion marked a turning point, for the time being, in the lengthy diplomatic correspondence.

Seven Western scientists and eight from Eastern Europe met at Geneva. This conference of technical experts, sometimes called the Technical Conference on Suspension of Nuclear Tests, met from July 1 to August 21, 1958. After thirty sessions, the group agreed that a workable and effective control system to detect violations of a worldwide suspension of nuclear weapons tests was feasible.[25] Western experts had called for 650 land-based control posts while the Soviet negotiations felt that 110 control posts were sufficient to provide adequate inspection. At the Geneva conference of experts, agreement was reached upon 160 to 170 land-based control posts, ten aboard ship, and inspection by aircraft.

One of the major problems facing the gathering of scientists was the detection of underground tests. The problem centered around the difficulty of distinguishing between earthquakes and underground tests. Agreement first centered around one kiloton, but was later revised upward to five kiloton. At five kiloton, the problem became somewhat less of an issue. Events not identifiable as coming from national causes were to be inspected.

Much of the ground work for the areas of discussion at the Conference of Technical Experts had been created by the Pugwash Conferences.[26] This term referred to a series of meetings attended by scientists from both the East and West. The first of these informal meetings took place in July, 1957, in Nova Scotia.

The United States and the Western powers were now ready to work on the administrative and political bases of a control system; however, to the Soviet Union, the fact that a control system was feasible meant that nuclear test cessation should be put into effect immediately.[27] On August 22nd, the United States and the United Kingdom suggested a second conference to begin on October 31st to negotiate suspension of nuclear weapons tests and to establish an international control system. The United States was willing to suspend tests on a year to year basis starting with the opening of the conference, provided that progress was being made toward the establishment of a control system and other arms control issues. Premier Khrushchev rejected these two conditions and forecasted the failure of the negotiations.[28]

The impasse which had developed between East and West was once again paraded before the world at the Thirteenth General Assembly Session that opened in September, 1958. The Soviet Union called for the immediate and unconditional halt to testing with no mention of control systems or of the findings by the Conference of Technical Experts. The draft resolution, put forth by the United States for the Western powers, called for cessation of tests under international control with no further tests after negotiations had begun.

Before the Geneva conference on cessation of nuclear weapons tests could begin, several new obstacles appeared to block the path toward any successful agreements. On October 1st the Soviet Union announced that it would resume testing. The United States had carried out a major series of tests during the spring and summer and the United Kingdom had also exploded nuclear weapons during this period. In the Soviet view, it therefore had the right to continue testing until their tests were equal in number to the Western nations.

The propaganda gain for the West was of short duration. On October 20th, France announced that it would not be bound by a United States, United Kingdom and Soviet Union test ban. Speaking for France was Jules Moch, a highly respected and well-known individual among United Nations delegations. Mr. Moch had once been called the "dean of disarmament" by one of the delegates. France took the position that it would not forego tests until the three existing nuclear powers agreed to halt manufacture of fissionable materials for weapons purposes and convert stockpiles to peaceful uses. The only question, Mr. Moch said, was whether France, from the point of view of its own interests, was right or wrong in equipping itself with nuclear weapons.[29]

The Geneva Conference on Cessation of Nuclear Weapons Tests

The Conference finally opened on October 31st. During the opening week the Soviet Union conducted three nuclear tests. Because of these the United States considered itself released of the pledge not to test.

During the first month of negotiations, the familiar deadlock once again appeared. Semyon Tsarapkin, who headed the Soviet delegation at Geneva, proposed a treaty for a test-ban before establishing a control system. The immediate purpose of the meetings, according to Tsarapkin, was the test-ban and not the control system, a position which was immediately rejected by James J. Wadsworth, the chief delegate of the United States at the Geneva talks. The prohibitions and limitations must precede the controls, from the Soviet point of view; however, after a month, an agreement was reached to enter into an immediate discussion of the control system. Since no agreement was reached on an agenda, the early discussions were held on an informal basis without a prepared agenda.

Before adjournment for the Christmas holidays, rudiments of a control system were agreed upon by the negotiating powers. Both sides agreed to the establishment of a seven-nation control commission to be headed by a single administrator. The United States, the United Kingdom and the Soviet Union were to be permanent members. The four other members were to be elected by the permanent members, and would serve on a rotating basis.

By the end of 1958, three major problems in the control field remained to be solved. The first of these concerned voting in the Control Commission. Tsarapkin insisted on the veto for the three permanent members. This would automatically include the dispatching of inspection teams since this function would be performed by the Control Commission. From the Western standpoint, a veto on substantive matters before the Commission would render the body ineffective.[30]

Disagreement also existed over the composition of the control commission. The Western proposal called for the United States, the United Kingdom and one ally, plus the Soviet Union, one ally and two neutrals to serve on the Commission. The Soviet Union suggested a Commission composed of the United States, the United Kingdom, and one ally, plus the Soviet Union, two allies and one neutral.

The second problem concerned the status of inspection teams. The West wanted permanent inspection teams which could be dispatched promptly. Soviet suggestions, however, called for the inspection teams to be created on an ad hoc basis. These teams would operate only in consultation with the nation being inspected and would be composed of nationals from that country. To the Soviet Union, permament inspection teams were a danger to the nation being inspected because of the possibility of espionage. In order to eliminate Soviet fear of espionage, the Western powers agreed to allow the country being inspected to conduct the team to and from the inspection sites. This latter attempt to solve the problem also met with failure.

The third point of disagreement involved the nationality of the inspectors who were to staff the control posts. As late as January, 1959, the West was insisting that the control posts located within the Soviet Union be staffed by a team whose personnel was fifty per cent from the West and fifty per cent from neutral countries. Those control posts located in Western countries would be staffed by half Soviet and half neutral personnel. The Soviet, in return, demanded that control posts be manned by nationals with two or three controllers from the other side. In June, the Soviet delegation increased the number of acceptable controllers from the West to six or seven; then in July the number was revised upward to ten. This Soviet offer was still considered inadequate by the West.

During July, the United States and the United Kingdom suggested that the control posts personnel be drawn one-third from the allies of the Western powers, one-third from allies of the Eastern bloc and one-third from the neutral nations. As mentioned above, the Soviet Union had made a concession in offering to allow ten controllers from the West to be included in the control post teams. The West had also made a concession by changing their demand from one calling for control post observers to consist of one-half from the East or West, depending on the location of the posts, and the other half from the neutral nations to a suggestion that the staffs be allocated on the basis of a three-thirds principle. Although the two sides had drawn closer together on the staffing of the control posts, no agreement on how the three categories of states would be determined was reached.

On December 14th, the Soviet Union offered to accept the Western three-thirds plan for staffing of the control posts and would also give up its demand for a veto over budget matters if the West, in return, would accept the 3-3-1 Soviet plan for the composition of the Control Commission.[31] The three powers had previously agreed to require a two-thirds vote for decisions on budgetary matters. Acceptance of the Soviet 3-3-1 formula would mean that one member of either the Soviet bloc or the Western group would have to join the other to muster the necessary two-thirds vote. This procedure would turn an obvious veto into a hidden veto. From the Soviet viewpoint, the Control Commission should be able to function only when there was agreement among the three permanent members. Under the 3-2-2 Western proposal, the United States and its allies could force decisions against the Eastern bloc.[32]

If the Western powers and the Soviet Union could not agree on where to begin in establishing a control system, how could agreement be reached on a solution to halt nuclear testing? Beyond this, it would seem ridiculous to suggest an approach that was supposed to lead to general and complete disarmament. Lack of agreement, at this time, on any significant part of a nuclear test ban, itself a partial measure, once again emphasized the fact that any arms control measure, to be successful, could not conflict with the national interests of the major parties involved in the negotiations.

From this point until after the presidential elections in 1960, the Geneva Conference on the Cessation of Nuclear Weapons Tests accomplished little. The General Assembly sessions were used by both sides to justify their positions before the nations of the world. The West continued to call for control measures while the Soviet Union used the sessions to urge cessation of nuclear weapons tests first, followed by consideration of the other problem involved.

The Technical Conference of Experts, which had met at Geneva from July 1st to August 21, 1958, agreed that any event that could not be identified as having come from national sources would be subject to inspection. Underground testing presented the most difficult problem, both from the technical as well as the political standpoint. Since nuclear explosions of low kiloton yield cannot easily be distinguished from earthquakes, a foolproof detection system would require on-site inspection. The 1958 Conference came to the conclusion that, on the basis of existing data, the number of earthquakes which would be undistinguishable, on the basis of their seismic signals, from deep underground nuclear explosions of about five kiloton yield, would be from twenty to one hundred annually.[33]

Between September 12th and October 30th, 1958,, the United States conducted the Hardtack II experiment, a series of thirty-seven tests which were designed to check the difficulty involved in distinguishing between underground nuclear tests and earthquakes. The tests revealed that the Conference had underestimated the difficulty of identifying underground explosions. United States scientists now felt that nineteen kilotons rather than five was the threshold[34] or the yield below which it would not be possible to distinguish between nuclear explosions and earthquakes. Following the Hardtack II tests, the United States asked that the new technical data be considered. Soviet delegate Tsarapkin, however, refused the request, deeming it a step backward. At the same time, the Soviet accused the United States of trying to find an excuse to begin testing.

On April 13, 1959, President Eisenhower, in a letter to Premier Khrushchev, proposed a suspension of nuclear tests in the atmosphere up to a height of fifty kilometers while the political and technical problems associated with control of underground and outer space tests were being resolved. Such an agreement would not require the automatic on-site inspections that had been the major stumbling block in the Geneva negotiations. Ten days later, Khrushchev rejected the Eisenhower proposal as "a dishonest deal" and suggested an alternative plan to reduce the number of inspections. The Premier called attention to British Prime

Minister Macmillan's expressed opinion that it would be possible to agree to carry out each year a certain previously determined number of inspections on the territory of the Soviet Union as well as on the territory of the United States and the United Kingdom, and that the number of inspections need not be numerous.[35] The Khrushchev proposal was introduced into the conference by Mr. Tsarapkin, who informed the West that the Soviet Union would not ask for the right of veto over the dispatch of inspection teams within the quota.

President Eisenhower's atmospheric test suspension suggestion was based on the findings of Project Argus, a series of three tests conducted three-hundred miles in outer space. A follow-up letter by the President in May 1959, asked for early discussion of concrete measures for high altitude detection. Premier Khrushchev's affirmative answer[36] led to the creation of Technical Working Group I of the Geneva Conference on Cessation of Nuclear Weapons Tests. This group of United States, British and Soviet scientists met separately from the Conference. Within the short period of three weeks, the scientists had completed their work and on July 10, 1959 they submitted a ten page report to the parent conference.

Group I scientists recommended that five or six large satellites weighing several thousand pounds be put into orbit at a height of over 18,000 miles. Each satellite should carry instruments designed to achieve maximum reliability and range of detection of nuclear explosions. Equipment should be installed in the network of the one hudnred and eighty ground control posts as recommended by the Technical Conference of Experts. The Soviet Union accepted all of the suggested control devices but one. The so-called "backscatter" radar was rejected because of its ability to detect missile launching. To the Soviet leadership, this was more a Western espionage device than a necessity of the control system.

No such progress could be reported by Technical Working Group II, also created by the Geneva Conference on Cessation of Nuclear Weapons Tests, to study the problems involved in detection of underground nuclear tests. Scientists from East and West met during November and December, 1959, but failed to reach any final agreements. The decoupling theory, sometimes called the big hole theory, which dealt with the muffling of underground tests, was an example of the disagreements that appeared between the scientists of the Soviet Union and those of the United States and the United Kingdom. The Rand Corporation made an estimate that a three-hundred kiloton nuclear explosion could be made to look like a one kiloton nuclear explosion if the test was conducted in a soft type of soil and certain other conditions were met.[37] Soviet negotiations refused to accept Dr. Latter's theory. If they could disprove this theory, the United States could be accused of formulating a plot in order to wreck the test-ban talks; however, Dr. Latter, using Soviet equations, was able to prove his theory.[38]

The problem of on-site inspections is closely related to the problems involving the composition of the Control Commission and the inspection teams.

At this time the Soviet Union was insisting that the number of such inspections permitted annually be based on a politically negotiated decision and that the maximum number should not exceed three. By the Soviet plan, each participating state, regardless of size, would be subject to three annual inspections.

Western leaders welcomed the offer as a sign of Soviet willingness to negotiate, but the offer of three inspections was considered inadequate. President Eisenhower indicated that the United States decision on the number of inspections to be agreed upon must be based on scientific knowledge of the estimated unidentifiable events occurring annually. The United States had previously indicated that this would mean approximately twenty on-site inspections within the Soviet Union each year.

Another point of East-West controversy was the size of the area to be inspected. Soviet negotiators argued that an area of seventy-eight square miles was adequate for on-site inspection purposes. The United Kingdom, presenting the Western position, held that since seismographic calculations were not precise, ground and air inspection teams should be permitted to examine an area up to 195 square miles.[39] The two Western states announced that they would accept the seventy-eight square mile limit when the other three variables used in establishing the location of the seismic event—time, distance, and direction—were not too difficult to measure.[40] Once again, the Soviet delegation refused to give serious consideration to these points of disagreement. From their viewpoint, this Western approach was another attempt to breach the iron curtain. Since Soviet missile strength had not been safeguarded by hardening their missile sites at this time, the same problems mentioned by Professor Blackett still existed to a certain extent.

On February 11, 1960, President Eisenhower suggested, as an alternative to a complete test stoppage, that a limited treaty be agreed upon, which would exclude tests in those areas most difficult to control. The President called upon the Soviet Union to accept a treaty that would halt tests above ground, in the atmosphere, those in outer space which could be policed, oceanic tests and those underground tests which could be recorded. Under these conditions the West estimated that twenty on-site inspections would be necessary.[41]

Immediate Soviet reaction was that since the proposal called for only a partial ban and also because it would permit resumption of underground testing below the 4.75 threshold, it was in reality a step backward; however, on March 19, they agreed in principle to accept a limited treaty as well as a program of research directed toward the improvement of instrumentation for detection. The only condition attached was that the states participating in the treaty agree not to test underground for military purposes during the research period. The length of time suggested was from four to five years. The West, however, was still reluctant to talk in terms of more than one year.

President Eisenhower and Prime Minister MacMillan, meeting at Camp David toward the end of March, agreed to the underground test moratorium provided that, (1) a phased treaty was signed; (2) arrangements were made for a study of a control system for tests below the threshold of 4.75; and (3) settlement of other outstanding problems was completed.[42]

On May 11, 1960, just before the ill-fated Paris Summit Conference, scientists of the three powers sat down to discuss a joint program of research on detecting the smaller underground nuclear tests. The Conference recessed the next day to await the outcome of the meeting of the Big Three. Although the summit conference never really began because of the charges and counter charges, the advisory group of seismic experts from the United States, the United Kingdom and the Soviet Union met during the last weeks of May to discuss plans for a joint research program.

In general, however, after the summit failure, the Soviet representatives made little or no effort to bridge the remaining gaps between the East and West positions. More important, however, the Soviet Union did not terminate these negotiations. Even though the meetings continued following the Paris fiasco, the three states failed to agree on the research program as well as on the number of annual on-site inspections and the composition of the Control Commission.

When the Geneva Conference reopened on September 27, 1960, new proposals were presented by the United States and the United Kingdom. The two powers were ready to extend the moratorium on underground tests to twenty-seven months instead of the year to year basis. The second proposal was to set the number of control posts located on Soviet soil at twenty-one in accordance with the recommendations of the 1958 Geneva Conference of Experts. This number was later reduced to nineteen, but the Soviet refused to consider more than fifteen. The third proposal by the United Kingdom would allow two years after the treaty went into effect for the installation of the control and inspection systems. The West had previously proposed three years while the Soviet Union had favored four years. All three Western proposals were rejected without any counter-proposals being made by the Soviets.

When the Conference adjourned on December 5th, to give the new Kennedy Administration time to consider its position, the disagreements over control and inspection remained rigid. On March 21, 1961, when the meeting reconvened, the West offered to accept the principle of East-West parity in the composition of an expanded eleven member Control Commission. Soviet reaction to the new proposals was to call for a troika head for the Commission.

In an attempt to salvage the badly deteriorating conference, the United States and the United Kingdom presented a complete draft treaty incorporating the sixteen articles that had previously been agreed to by the three powers. In addition, eight other articles reflecting the Western position on questions still at issue were added. The expanded eleven member Control Commission was to consist of four members from each the East and West plus three neutrals. The Soviet call for a triumvirate head for the commission was rejected as a step toward deadlock by the United States and the United Kingdom. After studying the draft for nearly two months, the Soviet Union concluded that it was a handicap to progress.

Final deadlock developed in June, 1961. Premier Khrushchev on June 4th stated that unless the West accepted the "troika" principle for administering a test-ban, the Soviet Union would deem it necessary to merge the question of the test ban with the larger question of general and complete disarmament. When Soviet delegate Tsarapkin read the Khrushchev memorandum into the record of the 317th meeting at Geneva a week later, Arthur Dean of the United States stated that apparently the Soviet representative came "not to negotiate but to dictate."[43] This exchange of views seemed to end the usefulness of the Geneva meetings which had lasted for town and a half years. On July 15th the Western powers asked that the subject of a test-ban with effective international control be placed on the Sixteenth General Assembly's agenda.

Almost three years of an unpoliced moratorium had passed when the Soviet Union announced, on August 30th, 1961, its intention to carry out a series of atmospheric tests. Between September 1st and November 4th, approximately fifty tests were carried out, climaxed with the detonation of a nuclear weapon in the sixty megaton range.[44] The United States resumed underground tests in the fall of 1961 and atmospheric tests in the spring of 1962. In the summer of 1962, the Soviet Union began another round of testing.

In November, 1961, the three power talks resumed in Geneva. In a sudden turnabout, the Soviet Union presented a new draft agreement which provided only for national systems of detection with no provision for international control or supervision of a test-ban.[45] A draft treaty, introduced by the West, called for an international control commission with rights of inspection along the lines agreed to in principle by the Soviet Union as late as mid-1961.[46] The issue no longer was the degree of international control, but whether there should be any international control at all.

The Geneva Conference on Cessation of Nuclear Weapons Tests had finally ended in failure in January 1962 but negotiations were reopened in mid-March in a subcommittee of the new Eighteen-Nation Disarmament Committee.

The international tensions which have prevented agreement on arms control measures following World War II continued during the late 1950's and early 1960's. The Soviet Union and the Western powers continued to suspect each other of hostile intentions, and therefore looked upon each proposal put forth by the other as an attempt to gain an advantage in the arms control negotiations. Mutual trust, mentioned earlier as the first essential for an agreement involving arms control, is still lacking.

International relations continued to rest on an unstable balance of military power. The assurance of security, which continues to be the chief purpose of arms control negotiations, was no closer to realization than before these negotiations were begun.

Eighteen-Nation Disarmament Committee

General disarmament negotiations had come to a standstill on June 27, 1960, when the Soviet side walked out of the Ten-Nation Committee.[47] At the Sixteenth General Assembly, agreement was reached on the resumption of these negotiations in an Eighteen-Nations Committee consisting of the members of the Ten-Nation Committee plus eight new members: Brazil, Burma, Ethiopia, India, Mexico, Nigeria, Sweden, and the United Arab Republic. Composition of the new committee reflected the Soviet desire for parity as well as that of the non-aligned nations to participate in the negotiations.

The opening date for the Eighteen-Nation Disarmament Committee was set for March 14, 1962. Before the Committee could hold its initial meeting, France withdrew from participation. Writing to Premier Khruschev on February 19, President DeGaulle stated that France wished to participate in any negotiations that could give hope of progress toward nuclear disarmament but that she believed negotiations should take place among the nuclear powers and that a ban on nuclear weapons tests without general disarmament would be useless.[48] The new Committee began its deliberations against the backdrop of recently completed Soviet nuclear tests and impending United States atmospheric tests.

In his opening speech, Foreign Minister Gromyko criticized the United States for deciding to resume atmospheric testing. He also reaffirmed the Soviet proposal of the preceding November for a test-ban agreement without international controls.[49] The Secretary of State, in his reply to Gromyko, called attention to the fact that the Soviet Union had broken the test-ban moratorium.[50]

During an informal discussion on March 15, the Western powers informed the Soviet Union that they were willing to make changes in their draft treaty. The most basic change offered was the complete elimination of the treaty threshold of 4.75 seismic magnitude on underground tests. This would mean that all underground tests would be prohibited by treaty and that there would be no increase in the number of control posts on Soviet territory or in the number of on-site inspections. It was also stated that most inspections would be conducted in highly seismic areas. This would eliminate most of European Russia from on-site inspections. These new proposals were flatly rejected. The Soviet position now was that not even underground tests required international controls.

A Subcommittee on a Treaty for the Discontinuance of Nuclear Weapons Tests, consisting of the United States, the United Kingdom and the Soviet Union, was established by the Eighteen Nation Disarmament Committee on March 21.[51] The new subcommittee had three proposals to consider. The Western plan envisioned an international control organization with worldwide international control posts and a limited number of on-site inspections by the international body, when it decided such an inspection was necessary.[52]

In reply, the Soviet representative accused the United States of adopting a completely unacceptable attitude toward the negotiations by submitting proposals which were aimed at obtaining unilateral advantages to the detriment of the security of the other parties. The Soviet proposal, still based on its November 28, 1961 pronouncement, called for an international control organization, with posts only in nations wishing to have them and on-site inspections only at the invitation of the nation to be inspected.

The third set of proposals, which had the backing of the neutrals, would provide for an international control organization, but with international control posts only in nations wishing to have them and automatic on-site inspection in only those countries taking part.

Mr. Godber, the United Kingdom Representative, in replying to Soviet delegate Tsarapkin's charge that the obstacle to agreement was not control but the unwillingness of the West to conclude a test-ban agreement,[53] pointed out that no matter what was said about the effectiveness of national systems, it could not be denied that disputes could arise over whether an explosion had actually taken place. The consequences then would be:

> ... if there were no international machinery to settle such a disagreement between the nations concerned, then any State which was suspicious that an event had taken place on the soil of another would be bound to claim that a test had in fact taken place and would itself feel free once more to test.
>
> There can be only one way of dealing with this situation. It is to have an international organization which will have inspection teams at its disposal; and such teams must have the right to go on the territory of the States concerned to decide, in the small area designated by the instruments ... whether this charge is justified or not. There is no reason why such visits of inspectors should not be limited to a yearly quota, but without any such basis of international inspection there can be no hope of a lasting treaty.[54]

Mr. Tsarapkin's reaction to the Mr. Godber's statement was as expected. The Soviet delegate felt that existing national systems of inspection were adequate for monitoring not only atmospheric, outer space and underwater nuclear tests, but also underground tests. He also argued that there had been comparable progress in methods of espionage:

> ... we know that methods of espionage are also being rapidly developed, especially in the United States, where various types of highly sensitive electronic apparatus have been evolved that are extremely suitable for intelligence and espionage activities.
>
> It would be sufficient to have a small group of technical experts who, if equipped with the appropriate instruments, could obtain highly important data revealing the defense system of the country in which they were stationed. We neither can nor will agree to this.[55]

The Tsarapkin statement obviously viewed the control deadlock only from the standpoint of detection. If detection were the only stumbling block, then an agreement could possibly be within reach. The problem of verification hinged on detection, as well as identification of suspicious disturbances in such a manner as to be able to distinguish between a natural phenomenon and a nuclear explosion.

When the Conference reconvened on July 16, 1962, following a month's recess, a new sense of urgency dominated many of the delegates who believed that a nuclear test-ban must be negotiated now or never. These fears and hopes were due to three main developments: (1) the eight nonaligned countries had made some positive suggestions which both the East and West were considering as a possible basis for negotiations; (2) the United States and Britain appeared ready to modify their views on the crucial issues of inspection and control on the basis of the results of a series of underground tests conducted in Nevada during 1962; and (3) both the West and the Soviet Union were aware of the fact that other nations, notably France and Communist China, were moving ahead with the manufacture and testing of nuclear weapons.[56]

The Western Powers' attention to the non-aligned nations underwent a marked change during this period. The change reflected a growing appreciation of the contribution the non-aligned members of the Conference could make in overcoming the stalemate that had been reached between East and West. Pressure by these eight nations on the West to reduce their demands in the area of inspection played a part in the formulation by the West of new proposals which were made public in August, 1962.[57] However, this influence was not nearly as great as some officials of the non-aligned nations would lead their readers to believe.

The early days, following the resumption of the Eighteen Nation Disarmament Committee, were marked by each side continuing to blame the other for the failure to reach an agreement. On July 21, the Soviet Government announced its decision to resume nuclear tests. The official statement concluded that since the United States had been first to conduct nuclear weapons tests, the Soviet Union reserved the right to be the last to end nuclear tests. At the twenty-second Subcommittee meeting on July 26, the Soviet representative further justified Soviet nuclear tests by claiming that in view of former President Eisenhower's statement of December 29, 1959, to the effect that the United States was no longer bound by the moratorium, the U.S.S.R. had been impelled to resume testing, particularly since "a whole number of facts showed that the United States was intensifying its military preparations in Europe, and in other parts of the world. . . . Moreover," he added, "France was systematically carrying out nuclear bomb tests in the Sahara. . . ."[58]

In reply, Ambassador Dean stated that President Eisenhower did not say that the United States would test, and in fact, the United States did not resume testing.[59] Ambassador Dean pointed out that Premier Khruschev, on January 14, 1960, had said that the Soviet Union would abide by its pledge not to renew its tests if the West did not resume testing, but on August 30, 1961, the same day that the United States and the United Kingdom had made new proposals to meet Soviet objectives, the U.S.S.R. announced that it would resume testing.[60] The United States delegate also recalled that the Soviet Union was the last to test before the moratorium began in 1958 and that it had also proceeded to carry out two tests after the Geneva Conference for the Cessations of Nuclear Weapon's Tests had begun, an action which the United States had chosen to overlook.

An Eight-Nation Proposal, put forth by the non-aligned members as early as April, 1962, also served as a source of disagreement between East and West. Both gave the appearance of accepting the proposal, but each side interpreted it to their own advantage. The United States and other Western representatives interpreted the memorandum as endorsing the principles of international control and on-site inspection. The Soviet Union, on the other hand, interpreted the eight-nation proposal in such a way as to make it practically coincide with its November 28, 1961, proposal which called for national systems of inspection.[61]

On August 1, 1962, President Kennedy announced in a news conference that on the basis of technical advances in the detection of underground tests, which were brought out in Project Vela,[62] the United States was prepared to accept national control stations which would be internationally monitored and supervised. The President, at the same time, emphasized that the new assessments did not affect the requirement for on-site inspection of all suspicious events.

At the twenty-third Subcommittee meeting on August 9, Ambassador Dean introduced modifications in the United States position on a comprehensive test-ban. These changes included an offer to cut by more than half the number of detection stations proposed to monitor a test-ban treaty and to accept the principle of nationally manned stations if the Soviets agreed to their supervision by the international commission.[63] The previous United States position had called for 180 internationally operated stations of which nineteen were to be located on the territory of the Soviet Union. Once again, the proposal was rejected by the Soviet Union. Mr. Zorin contended that the Vela data, plus scientific findings in other countries, confirmed that national detection systems were quite adequate.

Underground tests remained the chief stumbling block to agreement between East and West. From the Western viewpoint, these tests could be detected, but were difficult to identify because there were, at this time, no known seismic methods by which smaller nuclear explosions and small earthquakes could be positively distinguished. Using available detection methods, it was possible at this time to classify underground events into only two categories: (1) identified earthquakes; and (2) unidentified seismic events. For these reasons, the United States continued to maintain that on-site inspection was a pre-requisite to a comprehensive test-ban.

From a technical point of view, the actual number of on-site inspections required would be determined by the capability of existing seismic instruments, the number of earthquakes in an inspected region, and the feasibility of partially concealing explosions.

The banning of all tests, however, was clearly as much a political problem as a technical problem. The degree of assurance required by the West and the extent of on-site inspections that the Soviet Union would permit are essentially political questions. The Soviet continued to maintain that even without international control for underground tests there would be little danger of illegal testing inasmuch as existing national systems were capable of detecting nuclear explosions in any environment.

At the plenary session of the Eighteen Nation Disarmament Committee on August 27, the United States and the United Kingdom proposed two alternative draft treaties: (1) a comprehensive treaty providing for a total ban on nuclear testing in all environments based on internationally supervised, nationally manned control posts, and on-site inspections;[64] and (2) a limited ban which would end nuclear testing in the atmosphere, under water, and in outer space without the need to establish any international verification machinery.[65] President Kennedy and Prime Minister Macmillan, in a joint statement, emphasized their preference for the comprehensive approach, but if agreement on this treaty was not possible, then they were prepared to conclude a partial treaty.

Representatives of the United States and the United Kingdom pointed out that the proposals were consistent with recently publicized scientific findings and the principles of the eight-nation memorandum as well as the Mexican proposal of May 9, which had urged that a date be fixed for termination of nuclear tests. One of the reasons for presenting a limited treaty simultaneously with a comprehensive one was to take into account the wishes of the eight nations, who had urged this approach if efforts for a comprehensive agreement proved unsuccessful.

At the plenary and subcommittee meetings on August 27 and 28, Mr. Dean discussed the basic features of the two alternative texts. In regard to the comprehensive test-ban, even though its provisions marked a substantial departure from previous Western positions on some issues, the acceptance of the principle of obligatory on-site inspection still constituted the focal point for negotiations. The Ambassador pointed out that on-site inspection, based on an annual quota system, would occur only if unidentified events met the requirements for inspection as stipulated in the treaty; otherwise, there would be no on-site inspection. The draft treaty also left open for negotiation the number of on-site inspections which might be requested on the territory of any nation. Under provisions of the treaty, the signatory nations would not only be obligated to prevent nuclear explosions on their own territories, but would also refrain from encouraging or taking part in the conduct of such explosions anywhere.[66] These obligations were not to preclude the possibility of peaceful explosions which could be carried out upon the unanimous consent of the United States, the

United Kingdom and the Soviet Union.[67]

The comprehensive test-ban treaty also provided for an international scientific commission to consist of fifteen members with the United States, the United Kingdom and the Soviet Union as permanent members. The non-permanent members would include three from the Soviet bloc, two from the West and seven which were acceptable to both sides. Decisions by the Commission would be by simple majority of those present and voting.[68]

Among the powers of the body would be that of on-site inspection. The exact number of annual inspections to be permitted was not specified, but in territories of non-permanent members, the maximum was set at three per year. By a two-thirds vote, however, the Commission could specify a higher quota.

The budget, plus the choice of the Executive Officer of the administrative staff, must have the concurrance of the permament members. The proposal also specified that the Executive Officer and his staff were to be international in character and not subject to government instructions.

The Commission would also supervise the control arrangement in the verification system which would consist of: (1) stations built at agreed sites and utilizing superior equipment, but nationally maintained and manned and internationally supervised in accordance with specifications established by the international Commission; (2) stations based on those sites now in existence, but maintained nationally in agreement with the Commission; and (3) stations to be constructed and manned by the Commission on an international basis if deemed feasible and desirable. An important qualification to the comprehensive test-ban proposal would allow a party to withdraw if a state not party to the treaty conducted tests[69] or if the arrangements for on-site inspection had not been fulfilled. Withdrawal would not be effective until sixty days had elapsed from the date on which the withdrawal notice had been filed and the withdrawal notice would not be given until after a conference of parties had been held, or on a date sixty days after requesting such a conference.

The major features of the partial test ban proposal consisted of: (1) a ban on tests in or above the atmosphere and in territorial waters or high seas; (2) an obligation of the signing nations to refrain from encouraging or participating in such tests by other states; (3) permission to conduct peaceful explosions under specific conditions; (4) absence of any international verification machinery; (5) a termination date for testing; and (6) provisions for withdrawal. Western representatives rejected proposals that the partial test-ban be accompanied by a moratorium on underground testing. The moratorium would be contrary to the purposes of a partial test-ban. Cessation of underground tests required adequate and effective international control, and not merely a solemn pledge.

Soviet reaction to the two alternative treaty drafts was to allege that there had been no change from previous Western proposals. Despite Ambassador Dean's statement to the contrary, the Soviet representative claimed that the treaty drafts were not in line with the proposals of the eight-nation memorandum.[70] The

Soviet Union also opposed the partial test-ban on the grounds that it preserved the possibility of underground testing and would lead to unlimited experimentation which in turn would have the effect of legalizing nuclear weapons.

In response to Soviet Deputy Foreign Minister Kuznetsov's statement, President Kennedy, in his press conference of August 29, accepted the beginning of 1963 as a reasonable target date for the termination of all nuclear testing; however, at the same time the President rejected the idea of an unpoliced moratorium. Before the second session of the Eighteen Nation Disarmament Committee recessed on September 7, the Soviet Union accepted a United States proposal for continuing the test-ban negotiation. The three member Subcommittee continued to meet at Geneva while the parent Committee was in recess to permit the seventeenth General Assembly Session to consider the prospects for any agreement between East and West.

At the General Assembly Session, both sides used the meetings to gather backing for their position. The West called for a limited test-ban, excluding underground tests without international control. The Soviet Union replied by calling for the now familiar comprehensive test-ban on all but underground tests and a moratorium on these until agreement on a control system was achieved. Mr. Dean replied that the Soviet tests of 1961 had destroyed any chance that a moratorium would ever be accepted by the United States as a solution to the problem of nuclear testing.[72]

The United States agreed with the Soviet Union on the desirability of a total cessation of tests, but maintained that any ban must be verified by a control system including on-site inspection. During debate in the First Committee of the General Assembly, reference was made to several different figures for an annual quota of on-site inspections. The representative of the United Kingdom suggested that "perhaps one a month or even less" would do;[73] the New Zealand delegate suggested the possibility of having only one or two random inspections a year.[74] The Soviet Union once again rejected all proposals dealing with on-site inspection. Valerean Zorin's reply was to accuse the West of insisting that inspection was necessary solely for the purpose of supplying the North Atlantic Treaty powers with information for any future nuclear attack.[75]

Toward the end of 1962, a narrowing of the test-ban issues began to appear. This change, according to officials of the United States Arms Control and Disarmament Agency, came about because of several reasons. In the first place, the Cuban missile crisis of October, 1962, had put Premier Khrushchev in a tight position within the Communist world. By withdrawing the intermediate range missiles, Mr. Khrushchev had opened himself and the Soviet Union to criticism for backing down in the face of demands by the United States. The second reason, which is closely related to the first given by this United States official, was the competition between Mao Tse-tung and Khrushchev for the leadership of the Communist world. If he could reach some sort of agreement in the area of arms control or disarmament, the Soviet leader felt that this would be a help to him in his struggle with the Communist Chinese leader.[76]

In November the Soviet representative called attention to suggestions by Soviet scientists that automatic seismic stations be used to supplement national detection posts. These automatic stations, sometimes called black boxes, had been suggested as early as 1959 by American scientists but had been rejected by the Soviet Union. At the December 10 meeting of the Subcommittee, the suggestion was offered as a proposal by the Soviet Union. The proposal stated that it was prepared to agree to the establishment of two or three such unmanned stations on the territories of states that possessed nuclear weapons.

In a letter of December 19, Premier Khrushchev made the new proposal to President Kennedy. He claimed that Ambassador Dean, in informal talks with Kuznetsov at the General Assembly session, had indicated that the United States would accept an annual quota of two to four on-site inspections. The Premier stated that the Soviet Union was now willing to accept an annual quota of two or three inspections, along with the three seismic stations previously proposed. Earlier Soviet statements also indicated a willingness to allow a group of international scientists to visit the seismic stations and study their recording equipment to determine whether or not illegal tests had been conducted. This offer was conditioned on abandonment by the West of its insistence on international control posts and obligatory on-site inspection of unidentified seismic events.

President Kennedy, in his reply to Premier Khrushchev, indicated that he was encouraged that the Soviet Union now accepted the principle of on-site inspection, but felt that there had been some misunderstanding in regard to numbers. Ambassador Dean had advised the President that the only number mentioned in his conversations with the Soviet Deputy Foreign Minister, in regard to on-site inspection, was between eight and ten. Mr. Kennedy noted that this was a substantial decrease from the twelve to twenty inspections that the United States had previously proposed and he hoped that the Soviet Union would make some equivalent concession regarding its proposal of two or three inspections. Although the President questioned the locations proposed for the so called "black boxes," he did not feel that any of the problems were insoluble. At this point, he suggested that discussions between a Soviet representative and William C. Foster, the Director of the Arms Control and Disarmament Agency might be beneficial. Premier Khrushchev agreed to the proposed talks, but even though he was flexible on the locations of the automatic stations, this flexibility did not extend to the number of on-site inspections.

In the informal talks, which lasted from January 14 to 31, 1963, both sides agreed that a system of nationally owned and operated seismic stations would report to an international data collection center. The United States was no longer demanding international supervision of manned stations. It was also agreed that national systems would be supplemented by the automatic seismic stations. Even with these agreements, final agreement was impossible because the Soviet delegation, which included N. T. Fedorenko, the Soviet representative to the United Nations, and S. K. Tsarapkin, Soviet representative to the Eighteen Nation Disarmament Committee, insisted on an annual quota of only two or three inspections and no more than three automatic stations.[77] These talks were terminated at Soviet request and the whole problem was once again referred to the Eighteen Nations Disarmament Committee. Commenting on the results of the talks, Secretary of State Rusk felt that the Soviet Union might well be confident of its ability to find out about American tests, because the open nature of our society made it difficult to preserve secrecy.[78]

After a seven week recess, the Committee resumed in Geneva on February 12, 1963. The United States offered to agree on seven automatic stations and an equal number of on-site inspections.[79] It was also proposed to defer study of the number of inspections until agreement was reached on inspection procedures and the staffing of inspection teams. Views of the United States and the United Kingdom on these problems were summarized in a memorandum of April 1, 1963. This memorandum outlined a system of reciprocal inspection.

The Soviet Union, however, continued to adhere to the position which had been presented in the informal talks in January. Kuznetsov, the Soviet First Deputy Foreign Minister, once again declared that the number of on-site inspections and automatic stations was not subject to negotiation. The talks had become deadlocked, even though the two sides had finally reached basic agreement on the general nature of the control systems. Negotiations in the Eighteen Nation Disarmament Committee and in its three power subcommittee, failed to bridge the numbers gap during the first six months of 1963.

Test-Ban Controversy within the United States

Hope for progress was revived once again when it was learned that the United States and the United Kingdom were continuing their high-level correspondence with the Soviet Union. With the possibility of an agreement between the Soviet Union and the West, debate of the test-ban issue was greatly increased within the United States. Appearing before the Senate Armed Services Committee, William C. Foster stated that a test-ban treaty constituted the most likely first step toward control of the arms race. The failure to secure a test-ban treaty, according to Mr. Foster, could very well mean that we would be unable to place any limitations upon the race. A second risk of failure mentioned by the Director of the Arms Control Agency was that unlimited testing would, over a period of time, decrease the United States lead.

The risks involved, as Director Foster pointed out in his testimony, are primarily two:

the risk of undetected Soviet cheating, and the risk of secret preparations for testing followed by sudden abrogation of the treaty and an open resumption of testing by the Soviets. Of these two risks, Soviet cheating appears to be uppermost in the minds of many; however, based on this and past experiences with the moratorium, it is my judgment that the Soviet surprise abrogation is the greatest risk. A potential cheater could never know with assurance the exact threshold at which he could be sure of escaping detection from a particular site at all the many stations around the world on a particular day. He would therefore have to assume a lower threshold, if he wants to have some assurance of escaping detection, than those operating the detection system, who want to be sure to detect. . . .

The second risk in a nuclear test-ban treaty is that the Soviets would suddenly and openly abrogate the treaty after secret preparations for a test series. It is likely that a pretext could be found which might suffice to justify such a course of action for their propaganda purposes. If a test-ban were concluded we would make it a matter of declared national policy to maintain our readiness to test. Such a policy would, we believe, minimize the risk from surprise abrogation, although it would not prevent the Soviets from getting a head start in their testing program.

Cyrus R. Vance, the Deputy Secretary of Defense, indicated that the Air Force had been retiring large nuclear bombs in favor of smaller ones. Presumably no targets called for the larger bombs that could not be as efficiently eliminated with a number of the smaller weapons. Arguments that the national security of the United States depends on the big bombs fail when they are examined in terms of strictly technical factors that determine the effectiveness of a missile attack. In addition to explosive yield, the principal factors to be considered are the number of missiles, the overall reliability of each missile and the accuracy with which it can be delivered to its target.[81]

Admiral George W. Anderson, Jr., Chief of Naval Operations, testified before the Preparedness Investigating Subcommittee that the proposed test-ban treaty was acceptable only if certain deficiencies were corrected. These deficiencies included:

(1) the present draft treaty would prohibit all tests, including those which have essentially no probability of detection. This provision, which would prevent the United States from testing while providing the opportunity for the Soviets to test clandestinely, is considered to be the most significant deficiency of the treaty. Consequently, the Joint Chiefs of Staff have consistently taken the position that any test-ban treaty should prevent testing below appropriately specified and realistic detection thresholds; (2) the quota of seven on-site inspections would not provide a reasonable deterrent considering the number of suspicious events likely to occur in the Soviet Union annually. The number of inspections, however, is not the only consideration in determining the value of inspections as a deterrent to cheating. The quality of inspections is as important as the number.[82]

Dr. Edward Teller, of the University of California, disagreed with the proponents of a test-ban treaty, that the three chief advantages of such a treaty were: (1) such a treaty would make it more difficult for the Russians to catch up with the United States in the field of nuclear explosions; (2) the Russians were not prepared to perform the permitted underground experiments; and (3) the test-ban would slow down the proliferation of nuclear weapons. From Dr. Teller's point of view, there were several military disadvantages to the proposed test-ban. As cited before the Committee, these were:

> (1) the treaty could not be policed; (2) Russia would retain advantage in multimegaton explosives; (3) the treaty would inhibit the United States tests to verify the hardness of missile sites; (4) our missile defense would be impeded; (5) the language of the test-ban apparently prohibited the use of nuclear explosions in limited conflicts outside the territory of the United States unless a three month notice had been served in advance; (6) the treaty erected a new barrier against our cooperation with our allies in the area of preparedness, particularly in missile defense; and (7) by prohibiting certain types of experimentation the ban imposed limitation on future developments.

In place of a test-ban, Dr. Teller suggested that the Soviet Union and the United States agree not to put more than one megaton of fission products into the atmosphere in any one year.[83]

Dr. Harold Brown, the Director of Defense Research and Engineering of the Department of Defense, presented arguments to back the approval of a test-ban treaty. In testimony before the Subcommittee, Dr. Brown stated that:

> increasing the warhead yield at a particular weight in a particular vehicle by a factor of two gives it a greater effectiveness against a hard target. Keeping the warhead yield-to-weight ratio the same, which can be done without nuclear development, and increasing the payload capacity of the delivery vehicle by a factor of two, by improving the propulsive capability of its fuel, or by increasing its size, will have the same effect. But increasing the accuracy of the missile would also increase the effectiveness and might be the best way of the three to do the job.
>
> The Soviet technological advantage at the upper end of the yield spectrum has resulted from a considered decision by the United States not to concentrate effort in this field. Because of this, the United States is farther ahead at lower yields than the Soviets are at higher yields. There are uses for the hundred megaton bomb, but none of them appear very important. If need be, the United States can develop a fifty to sixty megaton devise without further atmospheric tests.
>
> Neither are atmospheric tests alone enough to develop an anti ballistic missile system. Other needs, such as improved radar and guidance systems are every bit as important.[84]

Dr. Norris E. Bradbury, the Director of the Los Alamos Scientific Laboratory of the University of California, located at Livermore, expressed concern over the ability to keep top scientists at these institutions as well as attracting new talent under the conditions which would prevail under a test-ban treaty. Testifying before the Preparedness Investigating Subcommittee on August 1, 1963, Dr. Foster also stated that key personnel had left because they felt that their talents could be used more effectively elsewhere.[85]

Dr. Bradbury, testifying at the same session, felt that failure to continue underground testing would be the greatest risk involved in a test-ban agreement. Even though underground tests would be permitted under terms of a limited test-ban, a reluctance to continue such tests could develop within the decision-making circle. If this were to happen, Dr. Bradbury felt that the United States would be in danger of falling behind the Soviet Union in the field of nuclear weapons.[86]

From the above, it is obvious that the controversy over a test-ban agreement existed not only between East and West but also among the top authorities within the United States. Military officials, for the most part, did not completely reject such an agreement, but all, including Admiral Anderson, Chief of Naval Operations, General Wheeler, the Army Chief of Staff, General LeMay, the Air Force Chief of Staff and the Chairman of the Joint Chiefs, General Taylor, insisted on stricter provisions relating to verification. Without an improved inspection and control system, the military refused to back the proposed test-ban treaty.

The feeling in some sections of the scientific community that not much more could be obtained in the way of tactical weapons improvements,[87] is not in accord with most expert opinion today. Technological advances have been more rapid during the 1950's and 1960's than in any other period of history. In the early 1950's, most discussion of defense against nuclear weapons assumed that these bombs were too valuable to be used on anything except large cities and top priority production targets. Few believed that the production cost could be decreased to a point where nuclear weapons could be used for tactical purposes. By the mid 1950's, a distinctive change appeared in the development of thermonuclear weapons.

As Kahn points out, technological progress has been so rapid that doctrinal lags are inevitable. These, in themselves, could lead to gaps in our preparations.[88] To labor under the assumption that these problems of arms control will be solved in an atmosphere of good will, while not making adequate preparations for resulting situations in case they are not, has the effect of placing the United States in a disadvantageous position from the standpoint of national security.

Limited wars, and the possible effect of a test-ban upon this type of war, was also the subject for many discussions in the Western camp. Only a comprehensive test-ban could have a drastic effect upon the Western potential to fight a limited war. Due to their limited size, the nuclear weapons needed for such a war could easily be tested underground. In this area of nuclear testing, the United States was far ahead of the Soviet Union.

The possession of the type of nuclear weapons needed to fight limited wars is an absolute necessity in today's world if the United States is to safeguard her national interests. By developing these weapons, a check is established against similar weapons developed by the Soviet Union. Possession of such weapons does not mean that they must be used, as some authorities argue. To introduce nuclear weapons in a limited war would break one of the major barriers to escalation of such wars. To date, a joint understanding as to the meaning of abstaining from nuclear weapons in limited wars seems to have been reached. There is no such joint understanding on the possible tactical uses of nuclear weapons.[89]

Test-Ban Agreement

The test-ban issue lay dormant from April to June 1963. During this period, however, Senator Humphrey and Senator Dodd, joined by thirty-two other Senators of both parties, submitted a resolution proposing an agreement to ban tests in the atmosphere and underwater, where testing could be monitored without on-site inspections of Soviet territory. If this resolution were rejected by the Soviet Union, it was suggested that the United States should publicly declare that it would not conduct atmospheric or underwater tests as long as the Soviets abstained from them. The resolution also stressed that the United States must be prepared if the Soviets suddenly resumed atmospheric or underwater testing.[90]

On June 10, President Kennedy announced in a speech at American University that the United States, the United Kingdom and the Soviet Union had agreed to high-level discussions in Moscow. These talks, it was hoped, would lead to early agreement on a comprehensive test-ban agreement. At the same time, the United States would agree not to conduct nuclear tests in the atmosphere as long as other states also refrained from testing.

The President stated that the test-ban treaty was the one major area where the end was in sight, and emphasized the importance of the treaty:

> ... While we proceed to safeguard our national interests, let us also safeguard human interests. And the elimination of war and arms is clearly in the interest of both. No treaty, however much it may be to the advantage of all, however tightly it may be worded, can provide absolute security against the risks of deception and evasion. But it can, if it is sufficiently effective in its enforcement and if it is sufficiently in the interest of its signers, offer far more security and far fewer risks than an unabated, uncontrolled, unpredictable arms race.[91]

In a press interview on June 15, Premier Khrushchev said that the President's speech was a step forward and stressed the need for finding ways to rid mankind of the arms race and the threat of thermonuclear war; however, the Soviet position on the verification needed for underground testing remained unchanged.[92]

The Eighteen Nation Disarmament Committee recessed on June 21 to await the outcome of the Moscow Conference. On July 2, Mr. Khrushchev expressed Soviet readiness to sign a treaty banning tests in the atmosphere, outer space and under water in conjunction with a non-aggression pact between the North Atlantic Treaty Organization and the Warsaw Pact Nations. He noted that the question of inspection did not arise, since the Western Powers had declared that no inspection was necessary for verifying compliance with a treaty limited to these environments.[93]

The limited test-ban treaty was negotiated in ten days. The American and British delegations were headed by Under Secretary of State Harriman and Lord Hailsham, while Foreign Minister Gromyko represented the Soviet Union. A non-aggression pact was not made a part of the treaty. Western powers opposed a formal treaty with the Warsaw Pact because they believed it would imply recognition of East Germany, a member of the Pact, and thus the acceptance of a permanently divided Germany.

On July 25 the test-ban treaty was initialed in Moscow by Under Secretary of State Harriman, Lord Hailsham and Foreign Minister Gromyko. The treaty was signed in Moscow on August 5 by Secretary of State Dean Rusk, Foreign Secretary Lord Home, and Foreign Minister Andrei Gromyko. After extensive hearings and three weeks of floor debate, the United States Senate voted eighty to nineteen for ratification of the treaty.[94] On October 7, 1963, President Kennedy signed the treaty and on October 10, it entered into force when the three original signatories deposited their respective instruments of ratification in each of the three capitals, Washington, London and Moscow. Over a hundred nations of the world have ratified the treaty.

The test-ban treaty prohibits nuclear weapons tests or other nuclear explosions in the atmosphere, in outer space, under water, or in any other environment where explosions would deposit radioactive debris outside the testing state. Signing parties also agreed not to encourage or cooperate with testing in any of these environments by other states.

The duration of the treaty is unlimited but any party may withdraw after three months notice if it decides that events related to the subject matter of the treaty have jeopardized its interests.

In the preamble, the original parties proclaimed their intention to seek "the speediest possible" agreement on general and complete disarmament and on the permanent discontinuance of all nuclear tests. No actual disarmament is called for by the treaty. No stockpiles are to be reduced, no weapons' production is eliminated, and not all nuclear tests are banned.[95]

Post Test Ban Negotiations

The nonaligned states, particularly those that were members of the Eighteen Nations Disarmament Committee, insisted that steps be taken quickly to facilitate the conclusion of a comprehensive test-ban. Some delegates suggested that the United States, the United Kingdom, and the Soviet Union initiate a coordinated program of seismological research and an exchange of information. It was also proposed that underground tests above a certain yield, which could be identified by national means, be immediately banned, and that the threshold be lowered progressively as the means of detection were perfected. These eight nonaligned nations also urged the nuclear powers to declare a two-year moratorium on all underground testing while negotiations continued on inspection, control, and detection.

Neither the Soviet Union nor the United States showed any interest in these proposals. The Western Powers remained opposed to any unverified moratorium on underground tests. Under these conditions, the General Assembly simply urged all states to become parties to the partial test-ban, and requested that the Eighteen Nation Disarmament Committee continue with its negotiations to achieve the objectives which are set forth in the preamble of the Treaty.[96]

During the 1964 meetings of the Disarmament Committee, the question of extending the test-ban was scarcely mentioned by either the Soviet Union or the United States. This attitude of the nuclear powers prompted the Nigerian delegate to remark that there seemed to be an agreement among the Big Three, and that the less said about disarmament problems at the time, the better.[97]

The United States and the Soviet Union seemed convinced that further test-ban negotiations at that time would do little more than confirm that their positions regarding verification were even farther apart than before the 1963 Moscow negotiations. The West continued to ask for seven seismic stations and an equal number of on-site inspections, while at the same time the Soviet Union still agreed to permit three automatic seismic stations and to accept the same number of on-site inspections. During the eighteenth General Assembly Session, the Soviets withdrew their acceptance of three on-site inspections,[98] and have since insisted that no special international control was required for an extension of the test-ban treaty.[99]

In September, the Eighteen Nation Disarmament Committee decided to adjourn until after the consideration of the arms control issue at the nineteenth session of the Assembly. The adjournment came at the time of a presidential election in the United States and the rapidly worsening Sino-Soviet-split. These made chances for agreement on problems of disarmament very unlikely. When the discussion failed to take place in the Assembly, the two co-chairmen, the Soviet Union and the United States, were unable to agree on resuming the work of the eighteenth Disarmament Committee in Geneva. Following this failure, the Soviet Union requested a meeting of the 114-nation Disarmament Commission.

The Commission, which consisted of all members of the United Nations, and which hadn't met since August, 1960, held thirty-three meetings between April 21 and June 16, 1965. In presenting its request, the Soviet Union noted that since all nations are affected by the disarmament discussion, these discussions should take place with all nations taking part. The United States agreed to the meeting, even though it felt that the smaller Eighteen Nation Disarmament Committee provided a more suitable forum for negotiations. These meetings of the Disarmament Commission revealed no narrowing of the differences between the United States and the Soviet Union on major issues. In his opening statement, Soviet Ambassador Fedorenko charged that the unwillingness of the United States to recognize the facts, namely, that national detection systems were adequate to control a ban on underground tests, blocked a solution to the problem.[100] Later Ambassador Fedorenko declared that the obstacles to agreement were political rather than scientific, and accused the Western powers of proposing technical studies which would confuse the issue and prevent people who were not scientists from expressing their views.[101] Speaking for the United States, William C. Foster, Director of the Arms Control and Disarmament Agency, replied that Fedorenko had merely repeated a non-negotiable position and that the Soviet Union was still unwilling to provide scientific proof for its claims.[102]

A resolution sponsored by twenty-nine states and adopted by the Disarmament Commission recommended that the Eighteen Nation Disarmament Committee reconvene as early as possible and that priority be given to extending the scope of the Test-Ban Treaty to underground tests. Albania was the only nation that voted against the resolution. The United States and all but one of the North Atlantic Treaty countries voted in its favor. The Soviet Union and nine other Communist countries abstained. These were joined by Algeria, Burundi, Cambodia, France, Guinea, Mali, Pakistan and Yemen.

The Eighteen Nation Disarmament Committee reconvened at Geneva on July 27, 1965. The United States and the United Kingdom still insisted that on-site inspections were necessary to distinguish between earthquakes and small underground tests. Ambassador Tsarapkin's first reaction was to attack the West for linking a ban on underground tests with a demand for international inspection and thus making agreement impossible.[103]

The eight non-aligned nations remained active in trying to find a solution to the impasse which had developed between East and West. Mrs. Myrdal, the Swedish representative, submitted a verification by challenge plan in early 1966. Under the plan, all underground testing would be suspended. Any party to the treaty who was worried about what appeared to be a strong indication that the treaty had been violated, but was still hesitant to ask for its abrogation, might challenge the suspected party to issue an invitation for inspection of the suspected area. If such a challenge were unheeded, the case for abrogation of the treaty would become particularly strong.[104]

As late as August, 1966, Mr. A. A. Roshchin, now the Soviet delegate to the eighteenth Nation Disarmament Committee at Geneva, reiterated that national means of identification were sufficient. Mr. Roshchin also stated that:

the proposal to control the banning of such tests on the basis of 'verification by challenge or invitation' is quite unacceptable to the Soviet Union, since it is designed merely to inject in a disguised form the concept of international inspections.[105]

This continues to be the position of the Soviet Union today.

As previously mentioned, the Nuclear Test-Ban Treaty does not in any manner deal with the use of nuclear weapons, their production, quantitative limitation or improvement by underground testing. Neither does the Treaty have anything to do with the design of nuclear weapons being developed in laboratories.

The Soviet goal of world Communism has not changed, even though the methods used may have altered. As Roswell Gilpatric, former Deputy Secretary of Defense emphasized—"the West must take precautions not to be lulled into a period of unpreparedness because of better relations with the Soviet Union."[106] Agreement, even on partial measures, can be expected only when the states involved feel that their national security is not jeopardized, and when each state feels that advantages to be derived from the partial measure are at least equal to the risks involved.

The goal of arms control and disarmament negotiations, according to some, is to accomplish disarmament in one mighty agreement.[107] At no time in previous history has this method met with success. The least comprehensive measures, which can deal with several aspects of the arms control problem, but which are not dependent on acceptance of the entire package of proposals, have the better chance of receiving approval by the world's major powers. This approach is exemplified by the partial Test-Ban Treaty.

In comprehensive disarmament proposals, unilateral concessions are thought, by some, to be a method by which confidence and better relations can be built between the opposing sides. Under the partial method of arms control, small unilateral concessions would not have a profound effect upon the relationship of the negotiating powers, if not followed by the other side. This would not be true in the case of comprehensive disarmament talks. Any unilateral concessions by the West, especially in comprehensive disarmament discussions, would arouse suspicion and concern on the part of Soviet negotiators. Such concessions are usually looked upon by the Soviet Union as a sign of weakness, rather than an effort to reach agreement on vital measures of arms control.

Problems analyzed in this chapter, in regard to the Test-Ban Treaty, will also be included in other areas of discussions, such as the treaty dealing with nonproliferation.

FOOTNOTES

[1] The term "disarmament" is used loosely to include reduction, limitation, or control of arms. Some important "disarmament" proposals, such as suspension of nuclear tests, do not involve actual disarming. For this reason, most writers

prefer the term "arms control."

[2]United States Arms Control and Disarmament Agency, *Third Annual Report to Congress: January 1, 1963 — December 31, 1963,* p. 17.

[3]Arthur H. Dean, *Test Ban and Disarmament: The Path of Negotiation* (New York: Harper and Row, 1966), p. 81.

[4]*Ibid.*

[5]Earl H. Voss, *Nuclear Ambush: The Test-Ban Trap,* Chicago: Henry Regnery Company, 1963, p. 31. Also see David R. Ingbs, "Ban H-Bomb Tests and Favor the Defense," *Bulletin of the Atomic Scientist,* X (November, 1954), pp. 353—357.

[6]The Soviet resolution suggested that the United States be invited to desist from testing atomic and hydrogen bombs in the trust territories, compensate the inhabitants for property damage, and return them to their homes. UN Doc. T/L. 504, 13 July 1954, p. 2.

[7]Louis Henkin (ed.), *Arms Control: Issues for the Public* (Englewood Cliffs, N. J.: Prentice-Hall, Inc., 1961), p. 26.

[8]Statement of Harold E. Stassen, Special Assistant to the President for Disarmament, before the Subcommittee on Disarmament of the Committee on Foreign Relations. See U. S. Congress, Senate, Subcommittee of the Committee on Foreign Relations, *Hearings, Control and Reduction of Armaments,* 84th Cong., 2nd Sess., 25 January, 1956, p. 15.

[9]U. N. Doc. A/C. 1/783, 12 January 1957, p. 3.

[10]William Frye, "Disarmament in the United Nations: A New Chapter?," *Bulletin of the Atomic Scientist,* XIII (March, 1957), p. 91.

[11]U. N. Doc. DC/SC. 1/PV. 87 (18 March, 1957), p. 23.

[12]U. N. Doc. D.C/112, 1 August 1957, Annex 12.

[13]U. N. Doc. D.C/SC. 1/PV 122, 17 June 1957, p. 5.

[14]U. N. Doc. A/C.1/L. 175 and Rev. 1. September 1957.

[15]Department of State, *The Nuclear Test-Ban Treaty: Gateway to Peace,* Publication 7254, Disarmament Series 3, Washington, August, 1961, p. 15.

[16]Harold Karan Jacobson, "The Test-Ban Negotiations: Duplications for the Future," *The Annals,* (January 1964), p. 93.

[17]*New York Times,* 27 March 1958, p. 1.

[18]Voss, p. 149.

[19]*Ibid.,* p. 159.

[20]U.S. Congress, Senate, Subcommittee of the Committee on Foreign Relations, *Hearings, Control and Reduction of Armaments,* 85th Cong., 1st Sess., 9—10 January, 1957, pp. 1064—1065.

[21]U.S. Congress, Senate, Subcommittee of the Committee on Foreign Relations, *Hearings, Control and Reduction of Armaments,* 85th Cong., 2nd Sess., 12 March, 1958, p. 1390.

[22]*Ibid.,* pp. 1429—1430.

[23]U.S. Department of State Bulletin, Vol. 38, No. 982 (21 April 1958), pp. 647—648.

[24]State Department Bulletin, Vol. 38, No. 983 (28 April 1958), p. 680.

[25]U.N. Doc. A/3897, 28 August 1958, p. 20.

[26]Beckhoefer, p. 488.

[27]U.N. Doc. A/3904, 9 September 1958, p. 7. Statement by Premier Khrushchev.

[28]*Ibid.,* p. 9.

[29]U.S. Congress, Senate, Subcommittee of the Committee on Foreign

Relations, *United Nations Disarmament: A Survey of the Debate and Resolutions of the Fourteenth Session of the General Assembly (September – November 1959)*, 86th Cong., 2nd Sess., 22 February, 1960, p. 5.

[30]U.S. Congress, Senate, Subcommittee of the Committee on Foreign Relations, *The Geneva Test Ban Negotiations*, 86th Cong., 1st Sess., 25 March 1959, p. 5.

[31]Supra., p. 137.

[32]Conference on Discontinuance of Nuclear Weapons Tests, Doc. GEN/DNT/213, 14 June 1960, p. 10.

[33]U.N. Doc. A/3897, 28 August 1958, p. 24.

[34]*The Annals*, January 1964, p. 95.

[35]U.S. Department of State Bulletin, Vol. 40, No. 1038 (18 May 1959), p. 705.

[36]U.S. Department of State Bulletin, Vol. 40, No. 1041 (8 June 1959), pp. 826–827.

[37]U.S. Congress, Senate, Subcommittee of the Committee on Foreign Relations, *Hearings, Technical Problems and the Geneva Test Ban Negotiations*, 86th Cong., 2nd Sess., 4 February 1960, p. 14. Dr. Albert Latter, of the Rand Corporation, developed the decoupling theory. For a detailed discussion of the technical problems involved in detecting and identifying underground nuclear tests, see U.S. Congress, Joint Committee on Atomic Energy, Congress of the United States, *Hearings, Developments in Technical Capabilities for Detecting and Identifying Nuclear Weapons Tests*, 88th Cong., 1st Sess., 5–12 March 1963.

[38]Voss, p. 342.

[39]For an example of the opposing points of view in the United States, see Hans A. Bethe and Edward Teller, "The Future of Nuclear Tests," *Headline Series–Foreign Policy Association*, No. 145 (January–February, 1961).

[40]Geneva Conference on Cessation of Nuclear Weapons Tests, Doc. Gen./DNT/PV. 205, 12 May 1960, p. 5.

[41]Arthur H. Dean, *Test-Ban and Disarmament: The Path of Negotiation* (New York: Harper and Row, 1966), p. 95.

[42]Bechhoefer, p. 500.

[43]*The New York Times*, 13 June 1961, p. 1.

[44]A megaton equals one million tons of T. N. T.

[45]U.N. Doc. DC/203, 5 June 1962, (ENDC/11). Proceedings of the Eighteen Nation Disarmament Committee will also be found in the United Nations Disarmament Commission's Official Records.

[46]*Ibid.*, (ENDC/9), 21 March 1962.

[47]The Ten-Nation Committee on Disarmament had been established on September 7, 1959 after consultation among France, the Soviet Union, the United Kingdom and the United States. The Committee, consisting of five Warsaw Pact states: Bulgaria, Czechoslovakia, Poland, Rumania and the Soviet Union; and five members of the North Atlantic Treaty Organization: Canada, France, Italy, the United Kingdom and the United States, met at the Palais des Nations in Geneva. The Ten-Nation Disarmament Committee was not an organ of the United Nations, but was created outside of the World Peace Organization. This did not mean, however, that the Committee failed to work in close cooperation with the United Nations.

[48]U.S. Arms Control and Disarmament Agency, Disarmament Document Series, Ref. 227.

[49]ENDC/PV. 2, pp. 6–7.

[50]ENDC/PV. 2, p. 24.

[51]ENDC/PV. 6, p. 27. An agreement between the opposing sides at an informal meeting on March 20 was approved by the whole Conference on March 21.

[52]ENDC/SC.1/PV. 1, pp. 4−7.

[53]*Ibid.,* pp. 7−10.

[54]ENDC/SC.1/PV. 2, pp. 3−9.

[55]*Ibid.,* pp. 9−16.

[56]Vera Micheles Dean, "The United Nations in a Developing World (1962−63)," *American Association for the United Nations,* Public Affairs Pamphlet No. 319T (New York, 1964), pp. 11−12.

[57]Arthur S. Lall, *Negotiating Disarmament−The Eighteen Nation Disarmament Conference: The First Two Years, 1962−64* (Ithaca, N.Y.: Cornell University Press, 1964), p. 23. Mr. Lall had served as the Indian Ambassador to the Eighteen Nation Disarmament Committee.

[58]ENDC/SC.1/PV. 22, pp. 23−24.

[59]*Ibid.,* p. 32.

[60]ENDC/SC.1/PV. 22, pp. 32−33.

[61]United States Arms Control and Disarmament Agency, *Second Annual Report to Congress: January 1, 1962 − December 31, 1962,* Publication 14 (Washington: U.S. Government Printing Office).

[62]The most significant was a new underground detection system, using recording instruments which had been placed in deep shafts or oil wells.

[63]ENDC/9, 21 March 1962.

[64]The text of the proposed comprehensive test-ban will be found in Appendix I.

[65]For the text of the proposed limited test-ban, see Appendix II.

[66]ENDC/SC.1/PV. 24, pp. 4−5.

[67]*Ibid.,* pp. 13−15.

[68]*Ibid.,* p. 6.

[69]ENDC/58, 27 August 1962.

[70]ENDC/SC.1/PV. 24, p. 37.

[71]*Ibid.,* pp. 38−40.

[72]U.N. Doc. A/C.1/SR. 1255, 30 October, 1962, p. 3.

[73]U.N. Doc. A/C.1/SR. 1256, 1 November, 1962, p. 10.

[74]U.N. Doc. A/C.1/SR. 1255, 30 October, 1962, p. 16.

[75]U.N. Doc. A/C.1/SR. 1246, 12 October, 1962, p. 13.

[76]Interview with an official of the United States Arms Control and Disarmament Agency, Washington D.C., 16 June, 1966.

[77]U.S. Department of State Bulletin, Vol. 48 (11 February 1963), pp. 198−202.

[78]U.S. Department of State, Documents on Disarmament, 1963, pp. 28−29.

[79]ENDC/78, 1 April 1963.

[80]Testimony of William C. Foster, Director, Arms Control and Disarmament Agency. U.S. Congress, Senate, Preparedness Investigating Subcommittee of the Committee on Armed Services, *Hearings, Military Aspects and Implications of Nuclear Test Ban Proposals and Related Matters,* 88th Cong. 1st Sess., 7 May 1963, pp. 7−12.

[81]Jerome B. Wiesner and Herbert F. York, "National Security and the Nuclear Test-Ban," *The Strategy of World Order,* ed. Richard A. Falk and Saul H. Mendlovitz (New York: World Law Fund, 1966), Vol. IV, p. 34.

[82]*Ibid.*, 26 June, 1963, pp. 303—304.

[83]*Ibid.*, 12 August 1963, pp. 543—558.

[84]*Ibid.*, 22 August 1963, pp. 847—858.

[85]*Ibid.*, 1 August 1963, p. 395.

[86]*Ibid.*, 1 August 1963, p. 440.

[87]Hans A. Bethe and Edward Teller, "The Future of Nuclear Tests," *Foreign Policy Association*, No. 145 (January—February), p. 30.

[88]Herman Kahn, "The Arms Race and Some of its Hazards," *Arms Control, Disarmament and National Security,* ed. Donald G. Brennan (New York: George Braiziller, 1961), p. 120.

[89]Donald G. Brennan and Morton H. Halperin, "Policy Considerations of a Nuclear-Test Ban," *Arms Control, Disarmament, and National Security,* ed. Donald G. Brennan (New York: George Braiziller, 1961), p. 236.

[90]S. Res. 148, 88 Cong., 1st sess., 2 May 1963.

[91]Documents on Disarmament, 1963, pp. 215—222.

[92]*Ibid.*, pp. 222—228.

[93]*Ibid.*, pp. 244—246.

[94]Dean, *Test Ban and Disarmament: The Path of Negotiation,* p. 81.

[95]For the complete text of the Test-Ban Treaty, see Appendix III.

[96]General Assembly Res. 1910 (XVIII), 27 November, 1963.

[97]ENDC/PV. 187, 28 April 1964, p. 34.

[98]U.N. Doc. A/C.1/SR. 1312, 22 October 1963, p. 5.

[99]ENDC/PV. 186, 23 April 1964, p. 17.

[100]*United Nations, Disarmament Commission, Official Records,* 72nd meeting, p. 3.

[101]*Ibid.*, 87th Meeting, pp. 3—4.

[102]*Ibid.*, p. 9.

[103]ENDC/PV. 220, p. 11.

[104]ENDC/PV. 247, 10 March, 1966, p. 22.

[105]ENDC/PV. 286, (prov.), p. 7.

[106]Roswell Gilpatric, "Our Defense Needs: The Long View," *Foreign Affairs,* (April, 1964), p. 366.

[107]Jerome B. Wiesner, "Comprehensive Arms Limitation Systems," *Arms Control, Disarmament and National Security,* ed. Donald G. Brennan (New York: George Braiziller, 1961), p. 198.

CHAPTER V

NON—PROLIFERATION: A
SECOND EXAMPLE OF THE PARTIAL
APPROACH TO ARMS CONTROL

Following the signing of the Nuclear Test-Ban Treaty in August, 1963, efforts in the area of arms control centered around reaching an agreement to prevent the spread of nuclear weapons. Although the Soviet Union has often talked in terms of general and complete disarmament since the success of the test-ban negotiations, the emphasis of both East and West has continued to be directed toward reaching agreement on first step or partial measures.

An explanation should be made of the meaning of the terms dissemination and proliferation. Lord Chalfont, the British Minister of State for Disarmament, defines dissemination as the spread of nuclear weapons from one country to another. Proliferation is used to mean the spread of nuclear weapons from one country to another in addition to the capability to manufacture such weapons. In most works dealing with arms control, however, the term proliferation is usually used to include both of the above meanings.

The most obvious response to the dangers of the spread of nuclear weapons was the call for a nonproliferation treaty. This could vary between a simple treaty, formulated in very broad or loose terms, and a more complicated instrument including certain sanctions and security guarantees. Each stipulation added will undoubtedly make the acceptance of certain individual powers more likely, but at the same time, these additions will also add greatly to the difficulties of negotiation with other powers. A simple treaty had to be the first preoccupation of the negotiators. Verification must be reduced to a minimum, an action which would be impossible under a complex treaty. From this starting point, a more inclusive treaty might be negotiated over a period of time.

General Problems of Proliferation

The policy of the United States since the end of World War II, whether under Republican or Democratic administrations, has been to prevent the spread of nuclear weapons. As early as 1946, the Baruch Plan called for an international authority to own or control all dangerous atomic materials from the mines to the finished products.[1]

In March, 1956, the United States proposed that the Soviet Union join in trying to prevent the spread of nuclear weapons. President Eisenhower, in a letter to Premier Bulganin, suggested that production of weapons grade fuel for atomic and hydrogen bombs be halted and that all future production be used for peaceful purposes. At this time, the United States, having stockpiled nuclear materials for over eleven years, was in a somewhat better position than the Soviet Union. The cut-off proposed by President Eisenhower would freeze this American advantage. Moscow, backed by world opinion, rejected the United States proposal. Permanent inspections plus international ownership also posed major points of disagreement.

The first Western nontransfer measure was part of a package proposal submitted by Canada, France, the United States and Britain to the five-nation subcommittee of the United Nations Disarmament Committee on August 29, 1957.[2] It provided for a cutoff in the production of fissionable materials for weapons. Following the cutoff each party would undertake "not to transfer out of its control any nuclear weapons, or to accept transfer to it of such weapons," except under arrangements which would assure their use only for defensive purposes. On September 20, 1957, the Soviet Union proposed at the United Nations that an agreement be reached which would not allow installation of any atomic military units or any types of atomic or hydrogen weapons beyond their national frontiers. The proposal would also forbid the placing of these weapons at the disposal of any other states or military blocs.[3]

Beginning in 1958, Ireland sponsored several United Nations General Assembly resolutions to prevent further nuclear dissemination. In that year, the Irish delegation submitted a draft resolution to the First Committee which called for an ad hoc committee to be established "to study the dangers inherent in further dissemination of nuclear weapons."[4]

The Irish resolution was greeted by major opposition from France. Jules Moch announced that France would not renounce atomic weapons which other countries already had and which they continued to manufacture. The French representative also indicated that France would not consider any agreement reached at Geneva as binding unless France adhered to it at a later date under such conditions as might then be decided.[5]

The Irish resolution was, in effect, a call for unilateral pledges not to disseminate nuclear weapons. At one time, this type of attempt to prevent the spread of nuclear weapons could have been looked upon with favor; however, today the technology involved in the development of nuclear weapons is no longer secret.

By March, 1960, the outlook for steps toward successful disarmament measures seemed to be within the reach of the representatives of the East and West. On March 15th, the Ten Nation Committee on Disarmament, which had been established in September, 1959, after consultations among France, the Soviet Union, the United Kingdom and the United States,[6] met at the Palais des Nations in Geneva. The meeting climaxed six months of small gains that had given cause for optimism; however, in the area of preventing further proliferation of nuclear weapons, no progress had been recorded. During the month of February, France had exploded an atomic device in the Sahara. With the French nuclear test, a new member was added to the nuclear club. The test also cast a shadow over any possibility of reaching any type of agreement on nonproliferation. From this time, France looked upon any resolution which dealt with nuclear testing, or nuclear proliferation as being addressed to her without specifically naming the country, and therefore, voted against them.[7]

According to some experts at this time, eleven other states, including the People's Republic of China, had the technical capacity to undertake nuclear weapons programs. Eight others were limited primarily by a shortage of scientific manpower, even though they had the needed technical skills. At least six other nations were economically capable, but these lacked industrial resources and scientific manpower.[8]

At this early stage, arguments both for and against proliferation were already being heard. Those who feared the spread of nuclear weapons maintained that it would increase the likelihood of total nuclear war since the states that believed they had less to lose from a war than the nuclear powers of the period might be tempted to take excessive risks. The chance that an accident might trigger a major war, or that a limited atomic war might lead to an all out nuclear war, was always present.

One of the arguments in favor of proliferation centered around resentment against the nuclear club concept. At the Fourteenth General Assembly session, the Greek representative noted that unless the prevention of further dissemination of nuclear weapons was related to a plan for general disarmament, the existing nuclear monopoly would simply be transformed into a monopoly in which the nuclear powers would continue to produce and stockpile nuclear and thermonuclear weapons. This condition of inequality could not be accepted by the non-nuclear nations.[9] This unacceptable bipolarization approach could be remedied, according to some arguments, by the wider dissemination of nuclear weapons.

It would be most unrealistic to expect the non-nuclear powers of today to accept the status of second class industrial nations happily while those countries which possess the nuclear "know-how" continue to expand this knowledge, thus widening the technological gap which already exists between the nuclear and non-nuclear nations. If we are to hope for the nonproliferation of nuclear weapons, these smaller nations must be guaranteed access to the knowledge and materials needed in the nuclear, industrial world of the future. Without such a guarantee, which could include provisions for inspection and verification, these nations will be forced to begin their own nuclear development programs, which will not necessarily be subject to any arms control system of verification.

France joined those nations opposing further dissemination of nuclear weapons. In his statement of April 13, 1960, Moch expressed the fear that if an agreement were not reached soon, in future years the four atomic powers, whose maturity had been proven, would be joined by less mature nations.[10] France, while professing great fear of the future spread of nuclear weapons, continued to expand her own nuclear capabilities. This is an excellent example of how a nation will advocate popular programs only when such programs do not interfere with the national goals or security of that nation.

The Soviet proposal for general and complete disarmament of June 2, 1960, also included a ban on the transfer of nuclear weapons or information which was necessary for their manufacture.

During the 1960 period, a growing sense of urgency developed over the problems of proliferation. There were three areas of particular concern. With its fourth above ground test in the Sahara, France had become a full member of the nuclear club.

The People's Republic of China posed the second point for concern among the world powers. Although problems within the Communist world, plus the withdrawal of Soviet technicians from China, would slow their development of nuclear capabilities, the experts still felt that Red China would join the world nuclear powers no later than 1963.

In view of the United States' decision to retain control over nuclear armament assigned to the North Atlantic Treaty Organization, the fear of dissemination of nuclear weapons among the treaty powers was somewhat lessened during 1960. Even so, the United States did pledge five Polaris submarines to the Treaty Organization. Professor Henry A. Kissinger, of the Harvard Center for International Affairs, felt that the United States should encourage the creation of a Western European atomic force. The West could then negotiate the location of nuclear arms from a much more flexible position because any threatened member would feel protected by the voice it had in the control of the overall military establishment. Dr. Kissinger also pointed out that such a force would be a means to prevent the proliferation of national atomic forces, which was almost sure to happen if the trends present at the time were allowed to continue.[11]

The fifteenth Session of the General Assembly passed a stronger resolution, once again proposed by Ireland, which called upon producers and potential possessors of nuclear weapons to refrain from exchanges of information and materials that might facilitate the dissemination of nuclear weapons.[12] This resolution was adopted in plenary Session by a vote of 68-0-26. Eleven members of the North Atlantic Treaty Organization were among those who abstained in the voting. In explaining the United States abstention, the American delegate argued that the best protection against nuclear war was an adequate defense system. Further proliferation of atomic weapons might be required to develop such a system, but the ability to manufacture nuclear weapons would not necessarily be expanded. It was also noted that the Irish resolution called for "unverified commitments of an indefinite duration," an approach which was not consistent with the United States insistence on control arrangements for all disarmament agreements.[13]

By 1962, the proliferation problem had become more serious as France and the North Atlantic Treaty nations moved closer to full nuclear development. France had tested five nuclear devices. With these tests, it seemed that President de Gaulle could possibly reach his target date of 1965 for a French striking force equipped with nuclear bombs in the kiloton range.

Early in May, the five nuclear powered submarines promised to NATO by the United States were on station. These carried a total of eighty intermediate range Polaris missiles. Although the control of the nuclear warheads remained with the President of the United States, this move was an important first step in providing NATO with its own nuclear weapons.

Other nations added to the alarm felt by the non-nuclear nations. Predictions were being made that Red China would join the nuclear club within two years. The head of South Africa's Atomic Energy Board claimed that his nation also had the scientific knowledge, ability and potential to produce atomic bombs. Communist sources were hinting that Poland and Czechoslovakia would demand atomic weapons if the Federal Republic of Germany were to acquire them.

As early as 1957, Dr. Hans Morgenthau had warned of the dangers which would face the world if nuclear weapons development was allowed to spread. Appearing before the Humphrey Subcommittee of the Senate Foreign Relations Committee, Dr. Morgenthau pointed out that although the problem of an all-out atomic war was not yet acute, it was likely to become an acute problem in a few years time with the rise of more nuclear powers.[14] To emphasize his remarks, Professor Morgenthau cited an example.

Today if an atomic bomb explodes in the port of New York we know who only could have planted it and could use atomic retaliation in order to operate against it and the very fact that we know it and the very fact that we can use that retaliation prevents such an atomic bomb from being exploded by the Soviet Union. But what is going to happen if in ten years' time an atomic bomb explodes in the port of New York? Against whom are we going to use atomic retaliation? Against whom are we going to drop atomic bombs?[15]

A United States program for general and complete disarmament, which was submitted to the United Nations General Assembly on September 25, 1961, included a ban on relinquishing control of nuclear weapons to states not owning them and on the acquisition or production of nuclear weapons by such states. Provisions against the transfer or acquisition were also included in the United States treaty outline which was submitted to the Eighteen Nation Disarmament Committee on April 18, 1962.

The Soviet draft treaty on disarmament, which was presented at Geneva on March 15, 1962, also included provisions banning dissemination of nuclear weapons by the nuclear powers and acquisition by other states. Like the United States, the Soviet Union had also proposed nondissemination as a separate measure.

A resolution passed by the Sixteenth General Assembly contained the main substance of both the United States and the Soviet Union's plans for general and complete disarmament. The resolution, based on the Irish sponsored resolution of 1958, called on nations possessing nuclear weapons to conclude an agreement not to relinquish control or transmit information about these weapons to any non-nuclear nation. The resolution also specified that the agreement should be subject to international "inspection and control" and called on states not yet possessing such weapons to refrain from their manufacture.[16] The resolution passed by acclamation.

Sweden had also sponsored a non-nuclear club resolution. The resolution asked the Secretary-General to conduct an inquiry into the conditions under which nations would agree to refrain from becoming nuclear powers. International control was not mentioned.[17] The resolution was passed by a vote of 58-10-23. The United States and its NATO allies opposed the Swedish resolution on the grounds that until general disarmament was achieved, or until the political and military threats had disappeared, it would remain necessary for the United States to continue to give its allies the military support which was considered necessary for their collective self-defense. The Soviet Union and its allies voted in favor of the resolution.

Most replies in response to the Secretary-General's inquiry were non-committal and expressed interest only within the context of a general treaty to refrain from becoming a nuclear power, or as part of an agreement on general and complete disarmament. To everyone's surprise, several of the most vocal supporters of the non-nuclear club concept were lukewarm in their replies. Sweden, for example, expressed readiness to join a nuclear-free zone in Europe, providing a satisfactory agreement could be reached. If no agreement had been reached by the end of 1963, "the Swedish Government wished to reserve its right to consider the matter anew in the light of the circumstances then prevailing."[18]

Geographic Zones as a Nonproliferation Approach

The nonproliferation of nuclear weapons issue first came before the newly created Eighteen Nation Disarmament Committee in March, 1962.[19] From the military and political standpoint, nuclear free zones, as a form of arms control, would be of exceptional value to the smaller nations. This could guarantee that neighboring states would not be armed with nuclear weapons; however, protection against the threat or actual attack by one of the great powers could not be guaranteed. Without the participation of the nuclear powers in such a treaty, it would still be of value but not as great a value. Great power participation in zonal arms control agreements implies a large degree of agreement among these powers, at least on the type of system by which they pledge non-use of their nuclear arms in a defined area.[20]

Polish Foreign Minister Adam Rapacki presented a memorandum containing a modified version of his first proposal which had been put forth in 1957 and called for the conversion of East and West Germany, Poland and Czechoslovakia into a zone free of nuclear weapons.[21]

Stage I called for a freeze of nuclear weapons and of the delivery systems within the zone. In stage II, all weapons systems would be removed from the zone and conventional armaments reduced, both by the nation whose territory was immediately involved and by those which had stationed armed forces within the area.

The proposal was once again rejected by the West on the grounds that nuclear free zones should be a part of an agreement on arms control and not an introductory agreement before it, because this approach could upset the basic principle of balanced disarmament. The Rapacki Plan would have required the United States forces in West Germany to divest themselves of nuclear weapons while leaving the nuclear weapons located in the Soviet Union still intact. It would also have barred West Germany from ever acquiring nuclear weapons or the materials and information needed to produce these weapons.

The United States had consistently opposed the denuclearization of Europe. In reply to the original proposal, the United States stated that the proposal was too limited in scope to reduce the danger of nuclear war or provide a sound basis for European security.[22] The reasons, as stated, were:

(1) the proposal did not deal with the essential question of the continued production of nuclear weapons by the nuclear powers; (2) it did not take into account the inability to detect existing nuclear weapons; (3) it did not affect the major sources of power, the United States and the Soviet Union, and therefore its effectiveness would depend on the good intentions of countries outside the area; (4) it did not provide for balance and equitable limitations of military capabilities; and (5) it would perpetuate the basic cause of European tensions by accepting the division of Germany.[23]

The latest version of the Rapacki Plan, put forth on March 5, 1964, made no significant changes in the previous proposals.[24]

The creation of a nuclear free zone in Europe, since it concerns the great powers, the United States and the Soviet Union, in addition to Great Britain and France, as well as the NATO and Warsaw Alliance systems, could not be established without the full cooperation of the nuclear powers.

Proposals for the denuclearization of Africa have also been put forth in recent years. These seem to have stemmed from the French nuclear tests in the Sahara and the desire of the emerging nations not to become involved in local arms races or the military competition between the East and West. In December, 1960, several African states introduced a resolution in the General Assembly which called upon members to consider the continent of Africa as a denuclearized zone. The United States opposed several clauses of the resolution and abstained on the final resolution. The United States representative expressed concern that, having approached the problems of disarmament on a global scale, the African resolution might interfere with the overall plan of disarmament and that it might place a limitation on the right of self-defense in Africa, which had not been placed upon other states.

The African resolution passed on November 24, 1961 by a vote of 55-0-44. The resolution called upon member states to:

(1) refrain from carrying out or continuing to carry out any type of nuclear tests in Africa; (2) refrain from using the territory, territorial waters or air space of Africa for testing, storing, or transporting nuclear weapons; and (3) to consider and respect the continent of Africa as a denuclearized zone.[25]

At the Addis Ababa Conference of Heads of African States and Governments, in May 1963, the African states affirmed the principle of a nuclear free zone in Africa. In July, 1964, thirty-three African countries once again declared their desire for the denuclearization of their continent. In reaffirming these resolutions in 1965, the General Assembly expressed the hope that the African states would take the necessary measures to implement the denuclearization of Africa.

While the African nations might take the lead in calling for a nuclear free zone on their continent, conditions existing today would hardly make it possible for the entire continent to be included in such a zone. The Middle East problem, and the intense hatred between the Arab nations and Israel, make it highly unlikely that these nations would accept any zonal programs for arms control. The attitude of South Africa, in addition to the fact that the French testing grounds are in the Sahara, are other problems facing those who advocate a nuclear free Africa.

Nuclear free zones in the Far East have been proposed by both the Soviet Union and the Peoples Republic of China. In January 1959, Premier Khrushchev proposed a treaty banning nuclear weapons in a zone in Asia. The following year, Communist China's Premier Chou En-lai proposed a similar treaty. On July 31, 1963 Red China proposed a conference to consist of the heads of governments of all countries to discuss the prohibition of all nuclear weapons from an Asian nuclear free zone as well as similar zones in Central Europe, Africa and Latin America.

These proposals were rejected by the United States. From the Western viewpoint, nuclear weapons were as much a part of the security system in the Far East as they were in Europe. The establishment of a nuclear free zone would upset the military balance in the Far East in the same manner as it would in Europe. Measures directed only at nuclear weapons would be inadequate and would serve only to increase tensions and promote insecurity. The United States representative to the General Assembly, Charles Stelle, cited past Chinese behavior as an additional reason for opposing denuclearization of an Asian zone.[26]

The first success in the area of the nuclear free zone approach came about with the signing of the Antarctic Treaty on December 1, 1959. The Soviet Union, the United States and ten other nations, including those with territorial claims in the region, signed the treaty. Nuclear explosions, as well as all military measures, were prohibited. Also included in the treaty was a provision granting complete freedom of access at all times to any part of the area in order to verify that the agreement was being observed. The Antarctic Treaty provided for the denuclearization of that part of the world below the sixtieth parallel of latitude south.[27]

On January 27, 1967, the Treaty of Principles Governing the Activities of States in the Exploration and Use of Outer Space including the Moon and other Celestial Bodies, was signed by the major powers.[28] The United States Senate approved the Treaty in April, 1967. Since the areas involved in the two above mentioned treaties were uninhabited, the political problems present in most disarmament negotiations did not exist to hamper agreement. This is not to say that no problems existed. However, the complexity of problems involving inhabited areas is somewhat greater.

Although Latin America has not been faced with the problem of nuclear testing in the same manner as have other areas, there have been numerous efforts to create a nuclear free zone in this part of the world. In 1958, the Costa Rican representative to the Organization of American States presented a proposal for arms limitation to the group. The proposal called for a pledge not to manufacture or acquire nuclear weapons and not to buy conventional weapons from countries outside the area. Also included in the proposal was a provision for an inspection and control system. At this time, no agreement was reached on the proposal.

During the Cuban missile crisis of October, 1962, Brazil, Bolivia, Chile and Ecuador co-sponsored a resolution in the United Nations General Assembly which provided for a denuclearized zone in Latin America. This resolution received widespread support both from the Latin American countries and from countries outside the area. The move was also welcomed by Arthur Dean, the United States negotiator, in the debate before the General Assembly. Speaking for the United States, Mr. Dean stated that his nation would welcome regional arms control arrangements provided that they were freely arrived at by the participating states. Ambassador Dean also stated that in areas where nuclear weapons were not deployed, agreement to ensure keeping them out, with verification, would be an important contribution to the overall efforts to prevent the wider dissemination of nuclear weapons.[29]

Later, Cuba insisted that any Latin American arms control zone must include Puerto Rico and the Panama Canal Zone and must eliminate military bases in the overall area, including the big American naval base at Guantanamo. These conditions were unacceptable to the United States.

The next move involving Latin America came about in April, 1963. Five area nations, Bolivia, Chile, Ecuador, Mexico and Brazil, issued a declaration announcing their willingness to sign a multilateral agreement which would prohibit the manufacture, importation, storage, or testing of nuclear weapons or delivery vehicles. The remaining Latin American nations were asked to accede to the declaration. When the General Assembly met in the fall of 1963, it passed a resolution which expressed the hope that the Latin American States would initiate studies to determine the measures that should be agreed upon with a view to achieving the aims of the declaration.[30]

The vote on the resolution was 91-0-15. The Communist states, which in the past had supported the establishment of denuclearized zones, abstained. Cuba continued to maintain that there could be no commitment on a nuclear free zone unless the Panama Canal Zone and Puerto Rico were included. The United States, which had usually been opposed to the nuclear free zone proposals, supported the resolution of Latin America but pointed out the need for adequate inspection and the adherence of all states in the area if the resolution was to be successful.

The Preparatory Commission for the Denuclearization of Latin America, which came into being as a result of the resolution introduced in the General Assembly by the five Latin American nations in April, 1963, held its first session in March, 1965. Three working groups were established to discuss the details of a possible treaty, but it soon became evident that the same obstacles, met at previous meetings, were still present. Cuba refused to approve any treaty that failed to meet two conditions: (1) the United States must give up its naval base at Guantanamo Bay; and (2) the treaty's geographic area must clearly cover all territories in the Latin American area which were administered by the United States.

Three alternative courses of action remained open: (1) the acceptance of Cuba's terms, which the United States would not consider; (2) agreement on a modification of the Cuban terms; and (3) proceeding without Cuba. If this problem could be solved, the conclusion of a multilateral treaty for the denuclearization of Latin America would be near to realization.

The second session of the Preparatory Commission met in August and September 1965. At this meeting the Commission established a negotiating committee to discuss with the nuclear powers their willingness to agree to respect Latin America as a denuclearized zone.

When the Preparatory Commission met for its third session from April 19 to May 4, 1966, it considered the text of a complete draft treaty prepared by its co-ordinating committee—the first nuclear free zone treaty to be negotiated involving an inhabited area—as well as an alternative draft treaty submitted by Brazil and Columbia. The articles on which there was complete agreement would prohibit "the testing, use, manufacture, production or acquisition by any means whatsoever of any nuclear weapons,"[31] among those parties signing the treaty. The receipt, storage, installation, deployment, and any other form of possession would also be prohibited.

An agency of a general conference and a secretariat would be established to supervise the compliance with the obligations to ensure that nuclear materials were being used only for peaceful purposes. Special inspections could be carried out either by the agency or by the International Atomic Energy Agency under the procedures formulated by the General Conference. The contracting parties would also agree "to grant the inspectors full and free access to whatever places and information that may be necessary for the performance of their duties."[32]

The Commission's draft would be open to all Latin American republics and other sovereign states of the Western hemisphere which were south of latitude 30° north and any other states which had international responsibility for territories in the region. The Brazilian and Columbian draft treaty omitted this latter group.

The Commission's draft provided that the treaty would come into force when eleven nations had ratified the document, while the Brazilian-Columbian draft delayed enforcement until all eligible parties had ratified the treaty. Brazil opposed any treaty that did not include Cuba. The minority draft required the ratification of two separate protocols before the treaty would take effect. One protocol would oblige the five nuclear powers to respect the denuclearized status of Latin America and promise not to take the initiative in the use of nuclear weapons in any part of the territory included in the area outlined in the treaty. The second protocol would bind nations having international responsibilities in Latin America to respect the denuclearized status of the continent.

The Treaty for the Prohibition of Nuclear Weapons in Latin America was signed in Mexico City on February 14, 1967.[33] One year later, on February 14, 1968, the United States announced that it would become a party to the treaty, however, two major stipulations were included. The announcement stated that the territories of Puerto Rico and the Virgin Islands would not be recognized as included in the treaty. Secondly, aircraft carrying nuclear weapons must be allowed to use landing facilities in those countries granting such permission.

United States policy on denuclearized zones varies according to the area and the nature of the measures which have been proposed. The United States has taken the position that it would welcome regional arms control agreements which were freely arrived at by the states involved. Furthermore, it holds that some regional arms control problems could be solved without waiting for the major powers to reach agreement on arms control and that regional agreements could help prevent local arms races.

Each zone must be considered as a separate proposal. The United States usually took the position that in areas in which nuclear weapons already formed part of the security arrangements, an agreement directed only at nuclear weapons would create an imbalance and therefore increase rather than decrease tensions. In non-nuclear areas, the United States took the position that nuclear free zones could be a useful approach to halting the further spread of nuclear weapons, but to be effective, these agreements would have to include adequate provisions for verification, be drawn up by the states in the area and accepted by them, and include all the states of the area.

Even though showing a willingness to consider regional arrangements, the United States has not taken an active role in pressing for them.

The political problems of each area and their effect on any possible arms control measures must be taken into consideration by those advocating the creation of nuclear free zones. In some instances, it is necessary that these political problems be settled before there is any prospect of reaching an agreement; in other cases the arms control agreements might assist in bringing about a solution to the political problems.

The composition of the region must also be considered carefully when forming a nuclear free zone. What nations would need to participate for the agreement to be successful? What type of arms control measures should be proposed under the existing conditions? The major factor governing most of the answers to these questions remains the national security of the participating nations and the effect any disarmament or arms control measures would have upon this security.

The North Atlantic Treaty Organization and the Multilateral Force

Following agreement on the Test Ban Treaty in August, 1963, the two focal points of the arms control negotiations centered on efforts to extend the treaty to underground testing and to prevent further proliferation of nuclear weapons. During 1964 the most distinctive feature of these negotiations was the increasing effort to reach agreement on collateral measures that would contribute to a reduction of tensions.

The Eighteen Nation Disarmament Committee resumed deliberations in January, 1964. Early in the sessions, both the United States[34] and the Soviet Union[35] submitted lists of collateral proposals, most of which were nothing more than revivals of previous suggestions. Disagreement still centered around a treaty on the nonproliferation of nuclear weapons, the establishment of observation posts to help reduce the danger of war by miscalculation or surprise attack, and the conclusion of a comprehensive test ban treaty. In the area of proliferation, the Soviet Union continued to insist that the transfer of nuclear weapons or access to them should not take place either directly or indirectly through military blocs.[36] The Soviet proposal criticized the proposed North Atlantic Treaty Organization's multilateral force as being in flagrant contradiction of the idea of the nonproliferation of nuclear weapons.[37] The United States maintained with equal emphasis that the two were compatible since the multilateral force would not result in additional states gaining actual national control of nuclear weapons. An Atlantic alliance, armed with nuclear weapons, would have to obtain this armament from the United States. This poses the question of congressional reaction to such a program.

The Joint Committee on Atomic Energy drafted the needed legislation to authorize the transmission of nuclear information which was necessary for the development of defense plans to our NATO allies. Carefully prescribed safeguards were attached to this authority by the Joint Committee, along with the stipulation that the data supplied was not to include important information concerning the design or fabrication of nuclear components of weapons.[38] Nuclear sharing, under the above conditions, meant sharing certain kinds of information, but not the control of weapons as has been stated by the Soviet Union.

Continued pressure by European allies for a share of control over nuclear weapons had led Secretary of State Dulles to announce, in 1957, that the United States would establish nuclear arms stockpiles in Europe for use by the NATO nations. It was hoped that such a stockpile arrangement would make it unnecessary for the Atlantic alliance members to manufacture nuclear weapons. Some still feared, however, that the United States would be reluctant to use nuclear weapons in defense of Europe because this could bring the United States under nuclear attack.[39]

Nuclear proliferation continued to threaten NATO. When the stockpile approach did not satisfy all members, the United States turned to a program of providing nuclear warheads for the alliance. These were to remain under American custody but the weapons were to be deployed in accordance with joint planning of the alliance membership.

In 1960, Secretary of State Herter told the NATO Council that the United States would supply a force of five Polaris submarines by the end of 1963 if the European governments would work out an accord on the political control of the force and also contribute one-hundred medium range missiles to the force as a second component.

Speaking in Ottawa, in May, 1962, President Kennedy announced that the United States would assign five nuclear submarines to the NATO command. A year later, the nuclear force began to take shape with the assignment of three Polaris submarines and one hundred and eighty British V-Bombers to the Supreme Allied Commander of NATO. The British, however, reserved control of their V-Bombers in case of supreme national interest. From this point of development, little advancement was made toward the multilateral force concept of the Atlantic Alliance. Agreement between East and West has been prevented more by a Soviet condition first attached in 1958, which would prevent the stationing of nuclear weapons in the German Federal Republic and the German Democratic Republic,[40] than by the differences found between United States and Soviet proposals.

When it became evident that the deadlock remained at the Geneva talks, the United States proposed that the two powers enter into private discussions in order to seek agreement on terms of a nonproliferation treaty. As an initial starting point, it was suggested by the United States that both powers should declare their intention to withhold nuclear weapons from the control of other states. Both powers would also demand statements from other nations that they would not attempt to acquire nuclear weapons. Once again, the result was complete failure.

The Pugwash Conference scientists also expressed concern over the possibility that nuclear weapons would spread to other nations, despite the inhibiting influence of the Nuclear Test-Ban Treaty. Working Group II of the Conference, which met at Udaipur, India from January 27 to February 1, 1964, devoted most of its report to this problem. The scientists called for:

(1) all nations presently possessing nuclear weapons should jointly undertake not to transfer these weapons or technical information relating to them to any other state or group of states; (2) the government of each of the nuclear powers should take whatsoever measures may be open to it to discourage its nations with experience in the field of nuclear weapons technology from contributing to the development of the nuclear weapons capacity of any foreign power; (3) States which abstain from manufacturing or acquiring nuclear weapons should have their territorial boundaries guaranteed by the United Nations; (4) the United States and the Soviet Union should recognize a special responsibility for cooperating to make this guarantee effective; (5) the governments of the nuclear powers, in order to encourage the policy of initial example, should seek to limit the nuclear arms race by refusing to accumulate further atomic bombs and nuclear warheads until the agreement on general and complete disarmament has been reached; and (6) the scientists of nations which do not possess nuclear weapons have the responsibility of warning their governments and countrymen of the dangers arising from the further spread of nuclear weapons.[41]

One of the suggestions that came from the Pugwash Conference was new. This was the call for the two major nuclear powers to recognize their special responsibility in helping the United Nations to guarantee the boundaries of states which abstained from manufacturing nuclear weapons.

The Eighteen Nation Disarmament Committee adjourned on September 17, 1964, to allow the nineteenth session of the General Assembly to discuss the current disarmament problems. When these discussions failed to materialize, the two co-chairmen, the United States and the Soviet Union, were unable to agree on resuming the work of the Eighteen Nation Disarmament Committee at Geneva. Following this failure, the Soviet Union called for a meeting of the 114-nation Disarmament Commission. This group hadn't met since August, 1960. In presenting its request, the Soviet ambassador noted that since disarmament affects the interests of all states, it should be discussed by a body on which all states were represented. Although feeling that the smaller meeting at Geneva was a more suitable forum for arms control negotiations, the United States agreed to the meeting. There was considerable support for calling a world conference to conclude a convention renouncing the use of nuclear weapons.

The thirty-three meetings of the Disarmament Commission between April 21 and June 16, 1965, revealed no narrowing of the differences that existed between the East and West on the proliferation problem. The multilateral force, proposed by the North Atlantic Treaty Organization, remained the chief target of the Soviet Union. From their viewpoint, the establishment of a nuclear force within the Treaty Organization would mean that nuclear weapons would be allowed to spread and that West German militarists would gain access to these nuclear weapons. From the Soviet viewpoint, no more serious threat could exist to the peace of Europe and the world.[42]

William C. Foster stated before the Senate Foreign Relations Committee on February 22, 1965, that the MLF proposal had two objectives. One was to meet the normal desire of our European allies to have a part in the determination of nuclear measures for their defense. The second objective was to meet this desire in such a way that would not promote proliferation.[43] In this instance, the Director of the Arms Control and Disarmament Agency seems to have provided an answer to the Soviet charge before it was made.

Nuclear weapons and their place in the North Atlantic Treaty Organization pose a key question for United States policy. Those who advocate that the United States provide nuclear arms for its allies argue that there are advantages to an independent nuclear striking force in Europe. These suggested advantages would be:

(1) each NATO nation would have more flexibility of defense, having both conventional and nuclear weapons; (2) European fear of failure of the United States to retaliate against a Soviet nuclear attack or that the United States would over retaliate, thus destroying Europe, would be decreased; (3) nuclear weapons would create a feeling of true partnership in the Atlantic Alliance; (4) the balance of power would be destroyed in Europe without the nations having nuclear weapons; and (5) the possession of nuclear weapons by individual NATO nations would change the power relationship between the Western nations and Communist satellite countries.

In answer to the above arguments, those who felt it would be to the disadvantage of the United States to create an independent nuclear force in Europe cited the following reasons:

(1) acquisition of an independent nuclear capability could once again encourage unilateral policies which would weaken the Alliance; (2) by removing the American protective need, the demand for the withdrawal of American troops from Europe could follow; (3) the possibility of member

nations using nuclear weapons for their own national objectives, (4) alliance members might make reckless decisions because of backing by other members; and (5) the exclusive reliance on nuclear weapons could enhance the danger of total nuclear war.

Although the North Atlantic Organization is constructed upon American nuclear power, the United States has sought to prevent the spread of nuclear weapons. While employing its nuclear capacity to protect itself and Europe from the Soviet threat, the United States has recognized a mutual interest with the Soviet Union to limit the nuclear capabilities of other nations. An increase in the number of countries possessing nuclear weapons would not only increase the chance of war, but would also add to the problem of controlling the arms race.

United States Draft Treaty Proposal and Soviet Reaction

When the Eighteen Nation Disarmament Committee convened on July 27, 1965, the chief topics of discussion remained nonproliferation and the comprehensive test ban. The first specific draft treaty dealing with nonproliferation was brought before the Committee on August 17 by the United States. Provisions of the treaty called for the nuclear powers to agree

"not to transfer nuclear weapons to the non-nuclear nations either directly or indirectly through a military alliance" and not to "take any other action which would cause an increase in the total number of States and other organizations having independent power to use nuclear weapons."[44]

Non-nuclear powers would agree not to manufacture or receive nuclear weapons.

The Soviet Union lost no time in rejecting the United States draft treaty. Any approach that might give the Federal Republic of Germany access to nuclear weapons brought immediate Soviet rejection. Ambassador Tsarapkin remained unconvinced by the argument that since the United States would retain a veto over the firing of nuclear weapons assigned to NATO, there would in fact be no increase in the number of nuclear powers. Mr. Tsarapkin asked first whether the United States draft treaty would ban access to all such weapons both directly and indirectly. By directly, he meant through national ownership, control and operation. By indirectly, he meant access by means of a multilateral force type organization.[45]

In reply to Ambassador Tsarapkin's questions, Mr. Foster stated that the draft treaty would clearly prevent the transfer of nuclear weapons into the national control of any non-nuclear country. It would also prevent any non-nuclear country from acquiring ownership or operation of nuclear weapons through manufacture. Also prohibited would be the transfer of nuclear weapons into the national control of any non-nuclear country.[46]

Soviet Draft Treaty Proposal
and Western Reaction

A Soviet draft treaty, dealing with nonproliferation, was introduced at the twentieth session of the General Assembly on September 24, 1965. This proposal would

prohibit any nation from transferring nuclear weapons in any form, directly or indirectly, through third States or groups of States, to the Ownership or control of States or groups of States not possessing nuclear weapons.[47]

This proposed treaty was aimed specifically at NATO and particularly the multilateral force. It provided that the existing nuclear powers could

not transfer nuclear weapons, or the control over them or over their emplacement and use, to units of the armed forces or military personnel of States not possessing nuclear weapons, even if these units or personnel were under the command of a military alliance.

Reciprocal limitations would apply to non-nuclear states, which would agree not to receive nuclear weapons or assistance in their manufacture.[48]

The Soviet draft treaty received the expected cool reception from the West. One question, which still remains unanswered today, asks for an explanation of the arrangements which have been made within the Warsaw Pact for consultation on, or joint decisions about, the possible use of nuclear weapons. It is common knowledge that in recent years the Soviet Union has turned over various short-range missiles, capable of firing nuclear warheads, to its Warsaw Pact Allies.

From the viewpoint of the Western nations, the Federal Republic of Germany could in no way be considered a threat to the security of the Soviet Union or its neighbors. Rather, it was the Soviet Union, with its large military units in East Germany, plus the hundreds of missiles aimed at the territory of the Federal Republic, that gave West Germany a legitimate concern about its security.

United States-Soviet Differences

United States-Soviet differences centered on what constituted proliferation. If the definition meant an increase in the total number of states or organizations, including military alliances, having the power to use nuclear weapons independently, then the issue was adequately resolved by the United States draft treaty. To make American intentions clearer and more explicit, amendments to the draft treaty were submitted to the ENDC in March, 1966. These amendments pointed out the intention of the United States to retain a veto over the use of nuclear weapons by any collective organization such as the Atlantic Treaty Nations.

Under the amended text, states would be prohibited from transferring nuclear weapons into the national control of any non-nuclear weapon State or into the control of any association of non-nuclear weapon States.

Nuclear weapon states would further be obligated

not to take any other action which would cause an increase in the total number of States and associations of States having control of nuclear weapons.

Control in this case was defined as the

right or ability to fire nuclear weapons without the concurrent approval of an existing nuclear-weapon State.[49]

The United States proposal, which the American delegation frankly admitted had been borrowed from the Soviet draft treaty when submitting amendments to the original proposal,[50] would bar any transfer of control of nuclear weapons to any association unless one of the members of the association was a nuclear-weapon state and that member gave up its entire nuclear arsenal to the association. Thus, conceivably, if the United Kingdom or France abandoned its nuclear weapons, NATO could become a collective deterrent and there would be no increase in the number of power centers that had the right to fire nuclear weapons.[51]

The Soviet view of what constituted proliferation is much broader than that of the United States. From their viewpoint, proliferation would include the participation of any new state in nuclear weapons policy formation even though that state had no independent authority to use the weapon.

If we permit the transformation of a nuclear power into an association of nuclear States we automatically permit the spread of nuclear weapons to those States which, before joining a nuclear association, did not themselves have nuclear weapons at their disposal. ... Instead of, say five nuclear powers, there will be four nuclear powers and one nuclear association comprising, for example, fifteen States belonging to that association. There will thus be not five, but nineteen States having access, to a greater or lesser extent, to nuclear weapons.[52]

Too many loop-holes remained in the United States draft treaty, according to the Soviet delegation.[53]

During the spring and summer of 1966, negotiations in the ENDC remained deadlocked over Western insistence on retaining the European clause and Soviet demands that no loopholes exist which would permit the Federal Republic of Germany to have access to nuclear weapons. The "major sticking point" between the Soviet Union and the West, therefore, remained the question of the Federal Republic of Germany. The United States insisted that any treaty limiting the spread of nuclear weapons had to take into account existing commitments to its military alliances. The Soviet Union interpreted this position to mean that the United States wanted a nonproliferation treaty that would make an exception for Germany. Mr. A. A. Roshchin, the Soviet delegate at Geneva, speaking before the ENDC on June 14, 1966 stated that the danger to peace

> stems from West Germany which, with the support of the United States, is continuing along the path of the rebirth of militarism and revenge-seeking.[54]

In reply to the charge that the Soviet draft treaty was designed to destroy the effectiveness of NATO, Roshchin answered that the proposal

> pursues the objective of preventing the proliferation of nuclear weapons through military alliances such as NATO, but does not affect the alliances themselves in any way.[55]

The Roshchin statement was once again rejected by William C. Foster. Speaking before the ENDC, the head of the United States Arms Control and Disarmament Agency reminded those present that "the Federal Republic of Germany was the only nation which had voluntarily pledged itself not to manufacture nuclear weapons."[56] Failure of the Bonn government to state its case clearly has resulted in a belief in some quarters that the Federal Republic is maneuvering in hopes of obtaining nuclear weapons. The unilateral declaration by the Adenauer government remains a binding agreement upon his successors. By revoking this, the Kiesinger government, or any other West German government, would run the risk of losing NATO support in case of attack. When West Germany complains about discrimination in NATO's nuclear policy, she is, in reality, complaining about the weakening of the alliance. Contrary to the feeling in some circles, Bonn is more anxious to see a strong NATO than to increase her status by obtaining nuclear weapons.[57] Nuclear status and prestige are secondary goals. The chief concern of the Federal Republic is her national security and this can best be preserved by a strong Atlantic alliance.

From the German viewpoint, the MLF was a way of confirming the United States commitment to the alliance. Few German leaders looked upon this as a first step toward a national nuclear force. During the first fifteen years following World War II, the Adenauer government was largely excluded from decisions involving the nuclear weapons stationed on German soil. Even the locations and numbers of these weapons were kept from German officials. As the security of West Germany became more dependent on nuclear weapons, and in light of her exposed geographical position to Soviet attack, it seemed only natural that the desire to share in decisions on the use of nuclear weapons would increase.

A poll conducted in January, 1966, indicated that 22% of those interviewed wanted a co-determination of nuclear policy, 28% rejected the co-determination approach, and 50% had no comment.[58] In another study, conducted to see what arms control and disarmament measures might be acceptable to Europeans in

1966, 1971, and 1976, 15% of 141 Germans picked European institutions as compared to 11% that chose NATO. Seventy-two percent refused to choose, but indicated that they preferred to support both methods.[59]

It would seem, from the above studies, that the desire for nuclear weapons by the Federal Republic has been greatly exaggerated by some who have confused the wish for national security guarantees by Bonn with the desire for a national nuclear striking force.

One possible area of agreement came from a suggestion by Secretary of Defense Robert McNamara. The Secretary acknowledged, at least indirectly, that the concern over West Germany's access to nuclear force had to be met. The McNamara proposal suggested a consultation procedure within NATO which would give the Federal Republic a voice in nuclear decisions but which would keep nuclear weapons from German hands. The consultative position was not rejected outright by the Soviet Union, but Foreign Minister Gromyko condemned the idea in a speech before the Supreme Soviet.

These developments seemed to indicate that the United States might be abandoning plans that involved German ownership or possession of a nuclear weapon system.[60] At the same time, a decision was made within NATO to establish a permanent committee for consultation on the use of nuclear weapons; however, there was no guarantee that such a committee would be acceptable within the alliance as an alternative to an allied nuclear force. Even if this consultative arrangement were agreed upon, there was no evidence that the United States would drastically alter its draft proposal.

Disagreement within the Western Camp

Although the major emphasis has been placed upon East-West differences, there have also been differences among the Western nations. The Kiesinger government has made it plain that the success of measures for nondissemination of nuclear weapons is a secondary consideration among some top leaders at Bonn. West German officials have of late been stressing the point that a nonproliferation pact could be dangerous to German scientific progress. While disclaiming any desire to possess nuclear weapons, these officials state very clearly that West Germany's future in peaceful nuclear development must be safeguarded. A treaty acceptable to Bonn must protect vital security interests and permit a civilian atomic program. It is in this area that the United States has placed the emphasis in recent guarantees to the Federal Republic.

Within the United States Arms Control and Disarmament Agency, some officials tend to place a major share of the blame for the failure to arrive at an agreement on proliferation at the doorstep of the Federal Republic of Germany. One official stated that West Germany has felt that it was necessary to keep things "hot" in order to keep attention focused on Germany. In this matter, West German officials hope for eventual unification of their country.[61] The same official of ACDA pointed out that at present the Federal Republic has nothing to trade in the international game of give and take. If it were a nuclear power, the condition would be somewhat different.[62]

British delegate, Lord Chalfont, generally supported the United States Draft Treaty; however, he observed, shortly after the proposal was made public, that the language of Articles I and II left open one possibility which the British would prefer to see closed. This referred to the injunction against any increase in the total number of states and other organizations having independent power to use nuclear weapons.[63] Objections by the British to the United States draft treaty were eliminated when amendments to the original draft treaty were submitted to the ENDC on March 22, 1966.

Remaining Political Issues

The center of the problem of a political agreement with the Soviet Union, like that of preventing nuclear proliferation, lies in Europe, and in particular in the unification of Germany. If the North Atlantic Treaty Organization can be eliminated, or at least weakened, one of the major Soviet foreign policy goals in Europe will have been accomplished. Because of this, it became necessary for the United States to re-evaluate its multilateral force proposal and to determine how important it was to the future of the Atlantic alliance as well as to each individual member of the Organization. At this time, the MLF was shelved by the Johnson Administration.

There is no advantage in rejecting Soviet complaints simply because of past differences. By studying and evaluating objections to proposals dealing with a nuclear force for NATO, advantages of alternative courses will be brought to light, especially in the area of preventing proliferation of nuclear weapons.

The major problem facing the United States in this area lies in deciding between a nonproliferation treaty and the Federal Republic of Germany playing a more important role in the decision-making process of NATO. The solution to this problem, which is not an easy one, lies in finding a means by which the Western European nations will have a greater say in the use of nuclear weapons in their defense while, at the same time, the United States retains control of the weapons.

The Non-Nuclear Powers

As efforts continue to find some means to limit the spread of nuclear weapons, more attention must be given to the complex political and technical issues. At the same time that the diffusion of nuclear technology is rapidly increasing, the cost of fissionable production is decreasing.[64] The popular and now widespread program for developing the peaceful uses of atomic energy has contributed significantly to the relatively free dissemination of nuclear technology. William C. Foster stated, in an article appearing in the July, 1965 issue of *Foreign Affairs*, that

one of the central facts with which we have to deal is the very great overlap between the technology for peaceful exploitation of the atom and that needed for weapons programs.[65]

Attempting to curb nuclear proliferation is not necessarily universally popular. Each signatory to a nonproliferation agreement would have to surrender at least a part of its freedom in making military decisions. Nations are not driven toward the attainment of nuclear status by simple motives. Success in deterring them from this goal will involve political bargaining as well as long hard negotiations to reach compromise. Three basic reasons that may prompt nations to desire nuclear status are: (1) anxiety for their own security and the wish to introduce a stronger element of deterrence into their system of national defense; (2) a desire to share in the position of prestige and influence which possession of nuclear weapons is thought to confer upon the existing nuclear powers; and (3) a desire for greater autonomy.[66]

France, for example, built a nuclear striking force chiefly because of the prestige involved. China strives for greater advancement in nuclear weapons, not so much for offensive purposes, but rather to lend backing to their conventional forces. The Chinese atomic explosion of October, 1964, dramatized the prospect of the diffusion of nuclear weapons. At that time, India, even though it had the capability to develop nuclear weapons, indicated that it did not intend to do so.

Chinese possession of nuclear weapons, and especially the testing of her first H-bomb in June, 1967, creates the possibility of nuclear blackmail by the Mao Tse-tung group. In the hands of a non status-quo nation, nuclear weapons can be a formidable force to recast the political map of Asia at the expense of India and other Asian nations. Afro-Asian countries, who have been in the foreground in criticizing the nuclear programs of other nations, have been strangely silent about continued testing and development of China's nuclear capabilities. Some writers see in this a welcome to the end of nuclear monopoly by the so-called "white nations."[67] Because of these reasons, there is in India today a minority opinion favoring an Indian nuclear capability.

By early 1967, some Indian officials had taken a somewhat different stand. After announcing that his country had nuclear capability, Foreign Minister M. C. Chagla announced, on March 28, that India would utilize her nuclear capability for peaceful purposes. But, under questioning, Mr. Chagla stated that India would consider her own security "of paramount importance" in considering whether to sign any treaty blocking the spread of nuclear weapons. The Foreign Minister made this comment when asked by a member of Parliament if it would be safe for India not to produce a nuclear bomb while its enemy Communist China was moving toward becoming a full nuclear power.

India has reminded the rest of the world of its objections to the proposed nuclear nonproliferation treaty. The Indian Government wanted the rest of the world to know that it would have no other alternative than to make the bomb unless Washington and Moscow came up with a nonproliferation draft acceptable to India and other non-nuclear lands.

The question of how the land of Gandhi and Nehru could possibly undertake a nuclear weapons program is uppermost in the thinking of the Indian leadership. To those who want a nuclear program it is suicidal to allow abstract concepts of morality to decide political issues when the national security, and even survival, are concerned. The sin, so to speak, is not in acquiring nuclear weapons, but in using them. Those who do not want India to become a nuclear nation point out that her position in world politics has been made by projecting moral issues into these policies. If India should become a nuclear power, this group feels that her position in world politics would suffer a severe setback.[68]

One of the easiest ways to eliminate the urge for nuclear weapons would seem to be to guarantee non-nuclear nations against nuclear attack by threatening massive retaliation on the attacking nations. Actually, this method is already in effect in the form of the Warsaw Pact and NATO and, in all probability, has contributed in a high degree toward nonproliferation. To be most effective, such guarantees should not offer or spell out specific commitments. Explaining in detail what action is to be taken against an attacking nation would commit the nation giving the guarantee to a rigid reaction. In allowing for flexibility, any would-be attacker will only be able to estimate the retaliatory action that an attacker will encounter. This in itself, is a form of blocking action.

Under certain conditions, unilateral guarantees might also be a handicap to the prevention of trouble in the nuclear world. Less responsible governments who have been given guarantees against nuclear attack by one of the super powers might use their sheltered position for a more adventurous foreign policy. These governments would still have to be given such guarantees. The reason for such a program is to deprive unstable nations of nuclear weapons.

Relationship Among Nations

In analyzing the nature of the danger posed by nuclear proliferation, a distinction must be made between the relationship of Nth countries to the major nuclear powers and that of Nth countries to each other.

The fear that Nth countries may acquire the ability to draw the major powers into a nuclear war is based upon the possibility of a surprise nuclear attack by an Nth country upon a major power which would be unaware of the origin of the attack. This theory assumes that the nation which was attacked would retaliate immediately against its chief nuclear opponent, without first verifying the origin of the attack. With the addition of the People's Republic of China and France to the world's nuclear powers, along with the split that has appeared in both the Communist and Western Alliances, the possibility of an immediate, reckless, retaliatory attack without prior verification of the origin of the attacking nation has been greatly reduced.

As the United States and the Soviet Union increase their nuclear capabilities, the incentive for either to launch an immediate retaliatory attack is greatly diminished. Since the major powers' ability to strike back cannot be significantly diminished by even a direct attack upon them, the incentive to wait out an attack and to determine its extent and from what nation the attack was launched has been greatly increased. The hope of picking up the pieces after the major powers have destroyed each other would seem very remote today. The probability that the country which launched the attack would be discovered and subjected to overwhelming retaliation is indeed very high. The gains to be achieved are too problematical and the risk too far out of proportion for any such action.[69]

The major danger to world peace today is found in the relationship of Nth countries to each other. During the period when it is known that certain countries are in the process of developing nuclear weapons, rival nations will be under tremendous pressure to launch a pre-emptive conventional attack. Failure to do so would mean running the risk of future nuclear blackmail.

As the spread of nuclear weapons increases, the imbalances between rivals will also increase. If rival countries would acquire nuclear weapons at roughly the same time, the first to do so would be under pressure to launch an attack while the nuclear advantage was in its favor. Failure to do so could mean an expensive arms race in order to maintain the hard-earned advantage.

Possible Approaches and Problems Encountered

Renunciation of the right to develop nuclear weapons by potential Nth countries offers a possible solution to the proliferation problem, but there are also serious shortcomings in this approach. As pointed out above, the greatest probability of the use of nuclear weapons arises from the relationship of the Nth countries to each other. Under these circumstances, a small number of nuclear weapons hidden by an Nth country could have a very profound effect on the balance of power among the non-nuclear nations. Because of this possibility, it is unlikely that nations would be willing to renounce the development of a nuclear capacity without absolute assurance that clandestine operations would not be conducted by other countries. This type of assurance would require an extremely complex inspection system which would be capable of detecting any diversion of atomic materials from peaceful purposes to weapons construction.

The inability to guarantee against the illegal construction of a small number of nuclear weapons has led to a suggested remedy known as the "nuclear umbrella" agreement. This agreement would be negotiated between the major powers. It would allow each side to keep an agreed number of weapons, even under an arms control agreement. Because of this arrangement, a small number of treaty violations would not have a major upsetting effect. The inspection system would be sufficient to prevent a large scale violation of the agreement.[70]

Problems are also encountered in suggested nonproliferation approaches among the major powers. Such an agreement would not halt the independent development of nuclear weapons. As the number of nuclear nations increased, inspection would become more difficult, even to the point of becoming an impossibility.

When the United States and the Soviet Union finally worked out their differences in regard to a nonproliferation treaty, there was still no guarantee that the non-nuclear powers would accept such an agreement. Many of these nations see in both the United States and the Soviet Union's draft treaty proposals an attempt to perpetuate the special position now possessed by the nuclear powers. Eight nonaligned members of the Eighteen Nation Disarmament Committee have asked that measures to prohibit the spread of nuclear weapons be coupled with tangible steps to halt the nuclear arms race and to limit the stocks of nuclear weapons and the means of their delivery.[71] The non-nuclear nations will not agree to a treaty which places controls on them, while at the same time allowing the existing nuclear powers to continue with the manufacture of nuclear weapons and delivery vehicles.[72]

West Germany and Italy are especially worried over the possibility of a compulsory safeguards clause which would require all countries which do not possess nuclear weapons to open their civil nuclear plants to inspections from the International Atomic Energy Authority in Vienna. The chief fear is caused by possible industrial espionage by the multinational inspection teams. Some German spokesmen have gone so far as to argue that Germany's industry would come under Soviet control.[73]

At a news conference on February 21, the chief American disarmament negotiator, William Foster, pointed to congressional insistence on safeguards to ensure that civil nuclear powers do not engage in clandestine military activities, and also on the need for a universal system of safeguards. At the same time, Mr. Foster refused to say whether the United States was still insisting on the incorporation of such a clause in any treaty.[74]

The Soviet position on the safeguards question is also clouded. When asked his government's position on the safeguards issue, chief Soviet delegate Roshchin simply stated that nothing had been decided.

Any single nonproliferation proposal will meet with opposition from one source or another. One measure put forth is bound to be more favorable to some powers than to others. By using the same approach which was used in the test ban treaty negotiations, that of packaging several proposals together, a series of compromises might be worked out which would be acceptable to the nuclear powers as well as the non-nuclear powers. This concept of nonproliferation involves a slow, more deliberate approach, rather than an all or nothing approach.

Although the Soviet Union continues to advocate the general and complete disarmament route in the arms control negotiations, past agreements, such as the "hot-line" and the Partial Test-Ban Treaty are proof that the Soviets will agree to partial measures when they feel that these are to their interest.

A nonproliferation agreement, to be completely effective, must have France and the People's Republic of China as signatories along with the other nations of the world. This requirement is obviously an impossibility today; however, this fact should not detain those nations who are working for an agreement to prevent the spread of nuclear weapons. No arms control or disarmament agreement in the history of the world has been one hundred percent effective. For this reason, the partial, step by step approach, mentioned above, is to be preferred to the general and complete disarmament solution. Under the partial approach, allowance can be made for the failure of such nations as France and Red China to sign the treaty. This could be in the form of a withdrawal clause, as found in the Test-Ban Treaty.

The relative stability of Soviet-American relations, in the post World War II period, gives a certain amount of freedom to the smaller powers. If this nuclear stability has helped in stabilizing the world situation, why wouldn't an even more stable condition emerge if other potential enemies obtained nuclear weapons? In the first place, there is no assurance that the new nuclear powers would use these weapons in a responsible way. The new nuclear powers could also put the super powers in a position of carrying out a policy which they would rather avoid. In effect, this would make the smaller nuclear powers more dangerous than the super powers.[75]

New uncertainties, introduced into the conduct of international politics by the rise of new nuclear powers, could possibly reduce the willingness of the major powers to undertake commitments in distant parts of the world, thus making the management of crisis throughout the world much more difficult. The effect of nuclear weapons in new countries, such as Israel and the Arab states, would have an unsettling effect upon local conflicts.[76]

The rate of proliferation, as well as the locations in which it occurs, must also be taken into consideration. When the rate of proliferation is gradual, the amount of anxiety will be lower. A rapid rate of proliferation will allow less time to make necessary decisions. In discussing possible problems in regard to the different areas in which proliferation may occur, several questions must be asked:

(1) are the countries of the area revolutionary or conservative; (2) do the nations have delivery systems; (3) do the nations belong to different alliance systems; and (4) do the nations of the area have direct connections to tensions between the super powers.

From the above it can be seen that a world of many nuclear powers would cause extremely difficult issues of management. Today's international system is characterized by restraint due to a set of political circumstances. We should not expect this to be true in a world where nuclear weapons have been allowed to become an important part of many states' military armaments.[77]

The super powers have developed a capacity for flexible response which allows them to avoid confrontations. Under this condition, a certain amount of escalation can occur before the danger of nuclear war is reached. This would not be true if smaller powers also possessed nuclear weapons. The United States and the Soviet Union would both feel obligated to increase their nuclear armament in order to keep a distance between themselves and the new nuclear powers.

In today's world, the major danger, contrary to popular belief, does not come from the alliance systems of the larger powers or from the United States and the Soviet Union taking opposite sides in disputes among third parties. The greatest danger emanates rather from what some writers call the "gray areas" at the edge of the major alliances.[78] In this case, each super power could be involved with a state outside its alliance commitment, but which it could not alllow to be destroyed.

The management of power becomes nearly impossible in a world where nuclear weapons have been developed or obtained by several states. The different levels of nuclear development create greater instability among the involved nations. Restraints, which have been observed by the super powers, may not operate in a multinuclear world.

Identical draft treaties, dealing with nonproliferation, were introduced at the ENDC on August 24, 1967 by the United States and the Soviet Union. Rejection of Article III, which dealt with inspection by the Euratom Countries, by the Soviet Union resulted in another deadlock.

On January 18, 1968, a second identical draft treaty was introduced by the two super powers. For months, the treaty was debated with little evidence of progress. Eight months after President Johnson had sent the treaty to the Senate, that body gave its endorsement by an overwhelming vote of 83 to 15.

The long period of discussion by the Senate, plus the fact that it became an issue in the 1968 political campaign, has led some of the Nth Countries to question the sincerity of United States intent in regard to the nonproliferation treaty. Soon after the Soviet military action in late August, 1968, Mr. Nixon expressed the view that any consideration of the treaty at this time would be inappropriate. This gave the impression that the treaty was a concession to the Soviet Union.

In reality, it was nothing of the kind. The Senate found, once it began earnest consideration, that the treaty was essentially self-serving, in that: (1) it keeps the nuclear powers from sharing with non-nuclear nations the knowledge, skills or materials relating to nuclear weapon development; (2) it bars the small powers which ratify it from requesting or accepting nuclear weapons; (3) the treaty endorses the free development of nuclear energy for peaceful purposes among all nations. It also pledges the aid of the nuclear powers in such development and allows the peaceful benefits of nuclear tests to be shared with non-nuclear nations; and (4) the treaty calls upon the "have" nations to explore together ways of achieving disarmament.

Some point out that the treaty merely indicates a willingness to seek early talks aimed at possible, practical steps which could be taken to limit the escalation of the arms race. Those not in sympathy with the treaty point out that two of the five nuclear powers, France and Communist China, have not signed the treaty and have no intention of doing so. They also note that Israel, India, West Germany, Japan and Brazil, which could technologically produce nuclear weapons, are unwilling, at this time, to sign the treaty. At this time, eighty-nine nations have signed the nonproliferation treaty and twelve have ratified it, including Britain, so far the only nuclear power to do so.

Even without full endorsement, the fact that the United States, Great Britain and the Soviet Union have come to terms is a most important accomplishment, and also the latest example to prove that the partial measure approach to arms control and disarmament is the only possible method which will lead to success, even if on a limited basis.

FOOTNOTES

[1]Department of State, *The Nuclear Test-Ban: Gateway to Peace*, p. 2.

[2]U.N. Doc. DC/113, 11 September 1957, Annex 5.

[3]United States Arms Control and Disarmament Agency, *To Prevent the Spread of Nuclear Weapons*, Publication 26 (Washington: U.S. Government Printing Office, 1965), p. 3.

[4]U.N. Doc. A/C.1/ L. 206, 17 October 1958.

[5]GAOR: 13th Sess., 1st Committee, 953 mtg. 17 October 1958, para. 5.

[6]SUPRA., p.

[7]GAOR: 14th Sess., 1st Committee, 1059th mtg., 19 November 1959, para 18.

[8]Howard Simons, "World Wide Capabilities for Production and Control of Nuclear Weapons," *Daedalus*, Vol. 88, No. 3 (Summer, 1959), p. 395.

[9]Statement by the Delegate of Greece. GOAR: 14th Sess., 1st Committee, 1055 mtg., 16 November 1959, para. 18.

[10]Ten Nation Committee on Disarmament, Doc. TNCD/ PV. 22, 13 April 1960, p. 9.

[11]*The New York Times Magazine*, 8 March 1959, pp. 19, 76—79.

[12]General Assembly Res. 1576 (XV), 20 December 1960.

[13]GAOR: 15th Sess., 1st Committee, 1135th Mtg., 19 December 1960, paras. 31—32.

[14]U.S. Congress, Senate, Subcommittee of the Committee on Foreign Relations, *Hearings, Control and Reduction of Armaments*, 84th Cong., 1st Sess., January 1957, p. 1088.

[15]*Ibid.*, p. 1089.

[16]General Assembly Res. 1665 (XVI), 4 December 1961.

[17]General Assembly Res. 1664 (XVI), 4 December 1961.

[18]United Nations Doc. DC/201/ Add. 2, 2 April 1962, p. 70.

[19]*Supra.*, Describes the make-up of the ENDC.

[20]Urs Schwarz, "Inhabition Through Policy: The Role of the Non-Nuclear Powers," *A World of Nuclear Powers?*, ed. Alastair Buchan (Englewood Cliffs, N. J.: Prentice-Hall, 1966), p. 157.

[21]ENDC/C.1/ 1., 28 March 1962.

[22]Paul F. Power (ed.), *Neutralism and Disengagement* (New York: Charles Scribner & Sons, 1964), pp. 147—148.

[23]Documents on Disarmament, 1945—1959, p. 1023.

[24]Power, pp. 62–64.

[25]General Assembly Res. 2033 (XX), 3 December 1965.

[26]Department of State Bulletin, November 18, 1963, p. 798.

[27]Monthly Chronicle of the United Nations, IV, No. 2 (February 1967), p. 13.

[28]*Ibid.*

[29]Documents on Disarmament 1962, p. 1024.

[30]General Assembly Res. 1911 (XVIII), 29 November 1963.

[31]U.N. Doc. A/6328, 12 May 1966, p. 15.

[32]*Ibid.*, p. 22.

[33]*Monthly Chronicle of the United Nations,* (March, 1967), p. 15.

[34]ENDC/120, 21 January 1964.

[35]ENDC/123, 28 January 1964.

[36]ENDC/PV. 186, 23 April 1964, p. 15.

[37]ENDC/PV. 187, 28 April 1964, p. 19.

[38]U.S. Congress, Joint Committee on Atomic Energy, *Amendments to the Atomic Energy Act of 1954,* As Amended, House Report, 85th Cong., 2nd Sess., 1958.

[39]Robert E. Osgood, *NATO: The Entangling Alliance* (Chicago: University of Chicago Press, 1962), pp. 220–221.

[40]ENDC/123, 28 January 1964, p. 5.

[41]Report of Working Group II, Twelfth Pugwash Conference on Science and World Affairs, 27 January – 1 February 1964.

[42]U.N. Doc. DC/PV. 72, 26 April 1965, p. 36.

[43]U.S. Congress, Senate, Committee on Foreign Relations, *Hearings, To Amend the Arms Control and Disarmament Act,* 89th Cong., 1st Sess., 22 February 1965, p. 11.

[44]ENDC/152, 17 August 1965. For complete text of the United States Draft Treaty, see Appendix IV.

[45]United States Arms Control and Disarmament Agency, *To Prevent the Spread of Nuclear Weapons,* Publication 26 (Washington: U.S. Government Printing Office, 1965), p. 9.

[46]*Ibid.*

[47]U.N. Doc. A/5976, 24 September 1965. For text of Soviet Draft Treaty, see Appendix V.

[48]*Ibid.*

[49]ENDC/152/Add. 1, 21 March 1966. For complete text of Amendments to United States Draft Treaty, see Appendix VI.

[50]*The Christian Science Monitor* (Boston), May 16, 1966, p. 11.

[51]ENDC/PV. 250, 22 March 1966, pp. 5–10.

[52]ENDC/PV. 252, 29 March 1966, p. 6.

[53]*Ibid.*

[54]ENDC/PV. 264, (prov.), 14 June 1966, p. 18.

[55]*Ibid.*, p. 22.

[56]*Ibid.*, p. 25.

[57]Theo Sommer, "The Objectives of Germany," *A World of Nuclear Powers?,* ed. Alastair Buchan (Englewood Cliffs, N.J.: Prentice-Hall, 1966), p. 42.

[58]*Ibid.*, p. 52.

[59]Karl W. Deutsch, "Integration and Arms Control in the European Political Environment: A Summary Report," *The American Political Science Review,* LX (June, 1966), p. 360.

[60]See *New York Times,* 23 February, 27 and 30 April, and 7 July 1966.

[61]Interview with a Second official of the United States Arms Control and Disarmament Agency, Washington D.C., 16 June 1966.

[62]*Ibid.*

[63]William R. Kentner, "A Reappraisal of the Proposed Nonproliferation Treaty," *Orbis,* X (Spring, 1966), p. 139.

[64]For a study of the cost of producing nuclear weapons, see Leonard Beaton and John Maddox, *The Spread of Nuclear Weapons,* (New York: Fredrick A. Praeger, 1962).

[65]William C. Foster, "New Directions in Arms Control and Disarmament," *Foreign Affairs,* (July, 1965), p. 592.

[66]International Assembly on Nuclear Weapons, *A World of Nuclear Powers,* (Toronto: International Assembly on Nuclear Weapons, 1966), p. 4. Also see R. N. Rosecrance (ed.) *The Dispension of Nuclear Weapons* (New York: Columbia University Press, 1964), p. 4.

[67]Sisir Gupta, "The Indian Dilemma," *World of Nuclear Powers?,* ed. Alstair Buchan (Englewood Cliffs, N.J.: Prentice-Hall, 1966), p. 57.

[68]*Ibid.,* p. 58.

[69]Henry A. Kissinger, *The Necessity for Choice* (New York: Harper and Bros., 1960), p. 244.

[70]See Thomas C. Schelling, "The Role of Deterrence in Total Disarmament," *Foreign Affairs,* (April, 1962), pp. 392–406.

[71]ENDC/158, 15 September 1965.

[72]ENDC/PV. 240, 15 February 1966, p. 13.

[73]*Manchester Guardian,* February 23, 1967, p. 2.

[74]*Ibid.*

[75]Leonard Beaton, *Must the Bomb Spread,* (Baltimore: Penguin Books Inc., 1966), p. 22.

[76]Alastair Buchan, *A World of Nuclear Powers,* p. 8.

[77]Stanley Hoffmann, "Nuclear Proliferation and World Politics," *A World of Nuclear Powers?,* ed. Alstair Buchan (Englewood Cliffs, N.J.: Prentice-Hall, 1966), p. 92.

[78]*Ibid.,* p. 103.

CHAPTER VI

THE ARMS CONTROL AND
DISARMAMENT PICTURE TODAY

The purpose of this work has been the analysis of the arms control and disarmament problems facing a world of nation-states, the acceptance or rejection of proposed solutions to these problems by the different states, reasons for the failure to reach a comprehensive agreement and finally, what methods have or will in the future be most likely to meet with success.

The questions to be considered in analyzing the past efforts to reach agreement in the area of arms control and disarmament are: (1) the extent to which these have resulted in failure; (2) reasons for the failure; (3) conditions which would have been necessary for complete success as well as limited success; and (4) the nature and extent of the achievements.

In any solution concerning the possibility or probability of reaching an arms control or disarmament agreement, the system of nation-states, in which each state is sovereign, must be taken into consideration. In view of past efforts, there can be little doubt that the failure to date to reach a comprehensive agreement stems from the conditions previously mentioned, such as the failure to understand that the long range national security goals of the world states will, to different degrees, be in conflict.

In arriving at any conclusions concerning the problems to be faced in arms control negotiations it is necessary to realize that although such measures may seem, on the surface, to be primarily military in nature, political motives have, in fact, been important both for those supporting and opposing these measures. Successful arms control measures must be an integral part of a political settlement. The armament race, of itself, is but a symptom of the political conflicts that exist in the world today. Disarmament, therefore, is a symptom of the lessening or possibly the disappearance of this political tension.

Whenever the military aspect alone is the basis for discussion, these discussions soon end in failure. During the period of the League of Nations, the Permanent Advisory Commission for Military, Naval and Air Affairs played a major role in the early decision-making process of the organization. Like the Permanent Advisory Commission, the Military Staff Committee of the United Nations was also expected to play an important part within the organization. In both cases the predominately military make-up of these bodies prevented any type of agreement on possible arms control measures. The military, still laboring under the conception that the military aspect must be of first importance and

103

that any related political problems could only be solved following the solution of the military, refused to consider any type of compromise.

Many writers point to the Rush-Bagot Treaty and the Five Power Pact, which emerged from the Washington Naval Conference, as examples of successful arms control measures. It is necessary to point out that the Anglo-American agreement was possible only because of the lack of any significant political disputes between Canada and the United States. The Five Power Pact, however, was successful only as an arms control measure for a short period of time. Shortly thereafter, as the signatory nations found it to their advantage to reject the commitments made in the Pact, each did so, and continued with their naval building program. Once again it was proved that attempts to solve the problems associated with arms controls could not be of a lasting duration without similar agreements on related political problems.

During the post World War I period, the French were primarily interested in regaining the Saar Basin, Alsace-Lorraine and other territories from defeated Germany, as well as imposing a one-sided disarmament program on the defeated Central Powers. In the same period, Great Britain was chiefly interested in maintaining her position as the world's top naval power. These military problems overshadowed the accompanying political problems. Instead of attempting to reach an equitable and lasting solution, the allied powers, especially the French, were more interested in revenge. This meant that the military would play the dominant role in any arms control negotiations.

The post World War II period has also been plagued by the failure of many military leaders to realize the close relationship that exists between military and political problems; however, the extent of this failure has been somewhat less than that following World War I. In the nuclear test-ban negotiations, many top generals and admirals flatly rejected any type of nuclear tests cessation on the grounds that the military preparedness of the United States would suffer a severe set back. Other high ranking military leaders, such as General Taylor, Chairman of the Joint Chiefs of Staff, and Admiral Anderson, Chief of Naval Operations, while rejecting a comprehensive test-ban, gave their qualified approval to a limited test ban treaty. This approval was based upon the elimination of underground tests from treaty provisions, plus the demand that laboratories and testing sites be kept constantly alert for any possible further nuclear tests which might be needed.

Although advances have been made in educating the military as to the importance of related political problems to their chief area of interest, the failure of many to comprehend this, or at least to admit it, has prevented further advancement toward the solution of many of the arms control and disarmament problems which face the world today. In assessing any arms control proposal, it is necessary to consider both the military-strategic implications as well as the international-political implications. Agreement on over-all arms control and disarmament will prove too difficult to secure until the international atmosphere is improved by the settlement of such major political issues such as Germany and Vietnam. There is nothing, however, which prevents partial measures of disarmament, such as a nonproliferation agreement or regional arms control agreements, which require a minimum of international verification, from being agreed upon without delay. These partial measures, it is hoped, would serve as stepping stones to agreements on more complex arms control and disarmament measures.

Another problem which has prevented any major agreement in the area of arms control, and which is also closely interwoven with the political and military aspects is the defining of the national security goals of the world's nations, especially those of the major powers. The basic origins of world tensions, and therefore of the arms race, are the hostilities between nations and their conflicting national goals. Each nation must first be interested in its own national security. Few, if any, nations have the same national interests and goals; therefore, the national security of each will be effected differently by agreements and happenings throughout the world. The problem of yesterday, as well as that of today, is the adjusting of these differences, preferably by peaceful means, so that they are not at too great a variance with what the major powers deem to be in their security interest. These super powers can, and will on occasion, adjust their short range aims in order to reach agreement with each other. This can be done without drastic changes in their long range goals of national security. From this standpoint, it becomes obvious that only partial or limited measures of arms control will be acceptable. An attempt to formulate a plan for general and complete disarmament would necessitate a complete revision of the long range national security goals of the major powers, an approach which neither the Soviet Union nor the United States is willing to consider.

Arms control, as such, cannot solve these problems nor can such measures survive in the long run unless these differences are settled. Nearly all significant limited arms control measures are judged unsafe by one or more of the parties involved.

The Hague Conference was called by Czar Nicholas II, supposedly to discuss ways to halt the developing arms race. It soon became evident, however, that the actual motive for calling the Conference was to help Russia obtain one of her major national goals. During this period, Russia needed time to consolidate her position in the Far East. To accomplish this, a cut in military expenditures was necessary. At the same time Germany and France had begun a drastic build-up of their artillery capabilities. Since the Czar's treasury could not meet the added burden of financing a rearmament program at this time, his finance minister tried to obtain this national goal by persuading the other nations that it was time for an arms control program for the betterment of world relations.

National security goals today are no less important than at the time of the Hague Conference. The Soviet plan for balance after World War II was drawn in such a way as to be of benefit to her at the expense of the Western powers. Stage I was the primary stage. All foreign bases were to be dismantled within a two-year period. Under this approach, there would be no balance in arms control. Stage I would result in a favored position for the Soviet Union, both in military and political balance. If arms control should cease after this first stage, the United States would find itself without the nuclear arsenal upon which it relied as a deterrent force to the large armies possessed by the Soviet Union and Communist China. If both the Soviet Union and the United States agreed to reduce their military personnel by one-third, the Eastern bloc would still retain the same numerical lead that it possessed before the cuts were instituted.

If the West were to agree to the elimination of foreign bases, this would, in effect, remove the United States from the continent. With this accomplished, the Soviet Union would no longer have to fear NATO. Under these conditions, the Federal Republic of Germany would cease to be a strong ally of the West. The allied position in West Berlin would be impossible.

Arms control proposals, which are formulated to help a nation obtain its national security goals, are not limited to use by the Soviet bloc. The Baruch Plan was designed in such a way as to help the United States maintain her nuclear superiority while at the same time preventing the Soviet Union from obtaining the needed knowledge to become the second nuclear power.

Discussions on both the Nuclear Test-Ban Treaty and a nonproliferation agreement followed the same course, with each side striving to maintain and, if possible, to expand its control in the areas which were deemed vital to the national interest. In the nuclear test-ban negotiations, the Soviets first called for a comprehensive ban with little or no inspection or verification. The Western powers also advocated the comprehensive approach, but with a thorough system of inspection and control. At that time the limited test-ban represented the only major compromise agreement reached between East and West. The Soviet bloc did not obtain their goal of the inclusion of underground tests in the agreement, but neither were the Western powers able to have their inspection demand included.

In this instance, the two super powers were able to adjust and compromise on goals and interests involving their national security to the extent that an agreement was possible. Later, in 1968–1969, this also became true in regard to discussions on the possibility of a nonproliferation treaty. Soviet national security goals cannot allow a nuclear armed Federal Republic of Germany under any circumstances. By the same reasoning, the United States cannot allow the development of a situation in which West Germany would play a lesser part in the defense of Western Europe. Even so, compromise was reached on this partial arms control measure.

The national security interests and goals of the lesser powers will, at times, also play an important role in arms control negotiations. As previously stated, a high official of the Arms Control and Disarmament Agency said in an interview in June, 1966, that the Bonn government felt that it was necessary to "keep things hot" in order to keep attention on Germany in the hope that chances for reuniting the country would be improved. At the same time, the thinking in the United States was that the reunification of Germany could better be promoted through disarmament negotiations. This lack of agreement between allies, as to how the national interests and goals can best be achieved, has also served to hinder agreement in the field of arms control and disarmament. Here too, the major powers can, and often will, make adjustments to accommodate the smaller nations, especially those that are aligned with them in the so-called "cold war"; however, this once again applies to immediate aims and objectives and not to long range goals of over-all national security program. The short range approach and methods used to reach certain aims in the short run must be flexible in order to meet the immediate needs. Long range goals, however, will be found to be somewhat more rigid.

Both East and West must be realistic in their security objectives. Each must be prepared to accept some risks in implementing an arms control or disarmament system. The objective should be to find a security system less dangerous than the accelerating arms race, rather than to achieve a system capable of providing absolute security, a goal which is obviously unattainable. Agreement on this point made the Nuclear Test-Ban possible. Another case in point was the dropping of the multilateral force project for NATO by the Johnson administration in an effort to reach agreement on the nonproliferation treaty.

The validity and stability of any arms control or disarmament system will depend ultimately upon the same motives and factors that underlie the existing system today; namely the self-interest of the parties involved. Any proposed system of arms control must be judged by whether it makes it more attractive to the parties, in terms of their own interest, to maintain the system and its safeguards, than to disrupt it by resorting to violence and evasion. In appraising any plan, each party will compare its benefits and risks under the proposed plan with its prospects without the plan.

Before accepting any program of arms control, each nation must be satisfied on two issues: (1) if carried out according to its terms, how will the plan serve its security or other interests as compared to the situation without it; and (2) would possible violations of the arrangement entail undue risks to its security as compared to the situation in the absence of the arrangements. To be acceptable, any arms control or disarmament agreement must combine its limitations, safeguards, and remedies so as to satisfy both criteria for all participating parties.

Throughout the history of arms control and disarmament discussions, the negotiators have been faced with choosing between comprehensive disarmament programs, referred to today as general and complete disarmament, and the partial or limited programs. Proponents of general and complete disarmament argue that in such a comprehensive plan, all participating nations will find some areas to their liking. Those who support this course of disarmament fail to realize that such an overall or comprehensive plan will also include many sections which are objectionable to many nations. No nation, above all, no super power, will consider agreeing to a general and complete plan of disarmament, simply because parts of the program are satisfactory. If the package is broken into separate areas for negotiating purposes, we no longer have a series of areas, being negotiated separately, which in reality, are identical to the partial or limited measure attempt at arms control.

Although general and complete disarmament has been advocated by different groups throughout history, at no time has this type of agreement been voluntarily arrived at by the world's nation-states. Following defeat in times of war, the victors have imposed what amounted to a form of complete disarmament, usually referred to as penal disarmament, upon defeated nations.

During the Hague Conferences, each participating country was primarily interested in limiting the armaments in which it was lacking, while refusing to discuss limitation of those armaments upon which it relied for military strength.

The Five Power Naval Pact was no exception to previous arms control negotiations, although some writers point to the Washington Naval Conference as an example of a successful arms control agreement. Britain and the United States could not agree on the type and number of cruisers each should possess. Great Britain, with her world wide empire, emphasized the need for smaller cruisers and larger numbers. The United States, with a smaller overseas commitment but with greater distance between possessions, demanded larger cruisers, but fewer in number. Actually, the only significant agreement reached at the Washington Conference dealt with capital ships. As an example of limited agreements in arms control, the Five Power Pact, which dealt only with capital ships, was most limited in scope.

In today's world, the prospects for reaching agreement on a plan for general and complete disarmament are even more remote than during previous periods of history. With the advent of nuclear weapons, failure by one nation, especially one of the super powers, to abide by agreements reached would leave the partially disarmed nations at a tremendous disadvantage, possibly even to the extent of complete extinction. For this reason, inspection and verification systems must be more foolproof than ever before. Because of this, more details must be included in any treaty or agreement being negotiated. This very fact greatly reduces the possibility of arriving at any type of comprehensive disarmament accord.

The Test-Ban Treaty is thought, by many, to be an example of a partial or limited arms control measure. Actually, however, a comprehensive test-ban would be an example of a limited arms control agreement, since only nuclear testing would be involved. Since underground nuclear tests are not included in the Limited Test-Ban Treaty, it must be considered less than a complete, partial measure. No actual disarmament is called for by the treaty. No stockpiles are reduced and no weapons are eliminated from national arsenals.

Limited or partial measures, as mentioned previously, are more consistent with the retention by the nation-states of some control over the type and level of their armament. In the present state of world affairs, the need for armament is just as pressing as the need to take seriously the possibility and consequences of nuclear war. General and complete disarmament requires agreement in the areas in which the nation-states are most divided. Measures of this type require agreement on earlier stages before proceeding to the next stage and, therefore, are actually limited or partial rather than comprehensive in nature.

The least comprehensive arms control proposals, which can deal with several aspects of the problem but which are not dependent upon acceptance of the complete package of proposals, have the best chance of satisfying the desires of the major powers. Agreement can be reached in some areas while others will be rejected. Areas in which agreement has been reached can be put into force without waiting for accord to be reached on the entire package of proposals. The Test-Ban Treaty, once again, is an excellent example.

The goal of arms control is not necessarily the total elimination of all war, although such a goal would be desirable if possible to achieve. To attain such a goal would require a radical change in national outlooks, which at the present time seems to be an impossibility, or the general acceptance of international peace-keeping machinery for adjusting conflicting national objectives. Such an organization would have to deal not only with the United States and the Soviet Union, but also with such cases as Israel and the Arab powers as well as North and South Vietnam.

The essential foundation for negotiation on arms control and disarmament is the possession by both sides of respectable military strength. Arms control and disarmament remain as much a function of national security as of armament. From this standpoint, limited measures may open the way to general disarmament, although at present this seems doubtful, while at the same time they are of great value in themselves.

The failure to agree on a final solution to the problem does not suggest that an entirely new approach to arms control is needed. As long as two drastically different political systems exist in the world (and this has been true throughout most of history) the only workable approach will be the slow, deliberate, partial measure method. Nations of both camps are afraid of a quickly arrived at, comprehensive agreement which will leave them at the mercy of the opposite bloc. For this reason, there is little if any chance of a comprehensive disarmament or arms control agreement.

From the above, it becomes obvious that the broad-based, highly idealistic, general and complete disarmament approach will not work in today's world. In a world of nation-states, each state must place the retention of its national sovereignty at the top of its long range goals of national security. Under these conditions, any program which advocates general and complete disarmament presupposes the existence of a world government—a government with the necessary power to put into effect its directives at the expense of those states which disagree with these directives. In today's nation-state type of organization, no individual state—above all, no state that ranks as a super power—will agree to any change that could jeopardize its major national security goal, that of maintaining its national sovereignty.

In any comprehensive disarmament program, the participating states will be most willing to compromise in those areas which are of little interest to them and which have little or no effect upon the long range goals of their over-all national security. Even so, progress will be lacking because in general and complete disarmament negotiations each state must agree to the entire package of proposals. To deal separately with each area would, in reality, be arms control rather than disarmament or the limited and partial method. Although writers have devoted much time and space to what is termed general and complete disarmament, the reader will find that in most cases these comprehensive disarmament proposals are actually a series of limited or partial measures which can be negotiated separately, and therefore are not, in the real sense of the word, comprehensive disarmament.

It is clear, then, that the only possibility of reaching any type of an agreement in the area of arms control and disarmament lies in trying to promote partial, limited disarmament, usually referred to as arms control. Limited agreements will necessitate only minor changes in the long range goals of the participating nations, changes which can be agreed upon in the "give and take" negotiations that are exemplified by the Test-Ban Treaty. The identical draft treaties dealing with proliferation, which were introduced at the ENDC on January 18, 1968, by the United States and the Soviet Union are the latest examples of the partial approach to arms control. Article III, which deals with inspection, allows each nation to negotiate separate arrangements with the IAEA. This could possibly result in each nation simply reporting to the Agency.

This would not be true in comprehensive disarmament talks.

Any agreement in such negotiations would entail drastic revisions in the national security goals of most world states, especially the major powers. These super states will not enter into long-range comprehensive programs when there is no way of evaluating their long-range effects.